The Life and Work of
ALBAN BERG

Da Capo Press Music Reprint Series

MUSIC EDITOR
BEA FRIEDLAND
Ph.D., City University of New York

The Life and Work of

ALBAN BERG

WILLI REICH

Translated by
CORNELIUS CARDEW

DA CAPO PRESS • NEW YORK • 1982

Library of Congress Cataloging in Publication Data

Reich, Willi, 1898-
   The life and work of Alban Berg.

   (Da Capo Press music reprint series)
   Previously published as: Alban Berg: Leben und Werk.
   Reprint. Originally published: London : Thames and
Hudson, 1965.
   Bibliography: p.
   Includes index.
   1. Berg, Alban, 1885-1935. 2. Composers—Biography.
ML410.B47R3793   1981   81-7854
ISBN 0-306-76136-X   780'.92'4 [B]   AACR2

Alban Berg

The Life and Work of

ALBAN BERG

WILLI REICH

Translated by
CORNELIUS CARDEW

THAMES AND HUDSON
LONDON

For Helene Berg

CONTENTS

Contents

INTRODUCTION

Only a few months had elapsed since Berg's death when I was first permitted to make a comprehensive assessment of his life and work. At that time the aim was to present and introduce all the works that he himself declared valid, and to offer an equally complete collection of his writings; only a brief sum/mary could be given of the external course of his life. It was only possible to produce the book in the short time available— it was published early in 1937 by the Herbert Reichner Verlag in Vienna—because Theodor Wiesengrund Adorno and Ernst Křenek contributed some of the most important reviews of the works. Once again I would like to express my hearty thanks for the invaluable help of these two friends.

In the twenty/seven years that have elapsed since then, Alban Berg has become a 'classic of new music', and his compositions have been evaluated—with varying degrees of profundity and accuracy—in several monographs and numerous articles in magazines and collections. Very little has been written about this artist as a human being.

The following is a completely rewritten version of that first book—long since out of print—and in it I have tried above all to give an account, with as much authenticity as could possibly be achieved, of the human aspect of Alban Berg and of his high spirituality. To this end the exhaustive biographical part is seeded with numerous quotations from his letters and other writings, and three longer articles of his are added in an appen/dix. Even in the section devoted to his work I have only used texts that were written by the composer himself, or at least under his supervision and with his consent. Happily such texts cover all his major works, and complete authenticity can be claimed for this section as well. In all modesty then, I hope that this new book will contribute something to the under-standing of the man and artist of genius, Alban Berg, by presenting him in the only light that is worthy of him, namely the light of truthfulness.

WILLI REICH

Part I The Life of Berg

CHILDHOOD AND PERIOD OF STUDY

Alban Berg (full baptismal name: Alban Maria Johannes) came into the world on 9th February 1885 in an old Viennese residence in the first *Bezirk* (Vienna I, Tuchlauben 8). His father Conrad Berg (1846–1900), who was a well-placed salesman in the export trade, moved from Nuremberg to Vienna in 1867 and later received the rights of citizenship. His family tree contains royal Bavarian officials and officers. Alban's mother Johanna (Maria Anna) Berg (1851–1926) was the daughter of a Viennese citizen; her forbears came from Nordböhmen and Baden. Her father, the court jeweller Franz Xaver Melchior Braun, had a distinct gift for music; he could not read music, but played everything by ear on the piano. He also possessed an exquisite talent for drawing and invented designs for jewellery which have been retained in the family. The grandson inherited both these gifts.

From photographs of Conrad Berg it can be clearly seen that as far as appearance is concerned the composer had many features in common with his father. The following description is taken from a biographical sketch of Conrad Berg placed at my disposal by Hermann Watznauer, who was the great friend of Alban's youth, although he was ten years his senior. Watznauer's description not only confirms the physical like-ness but also indicates a profound and essential similarity between father and son: 'His pale face was uncommonly clean-cut and noble. His eyes were deep-set, and his unusually wide eyelids ended in a fine-swung curve under the striking brows, tinged with grey. His frame was tall and spare; one could never have guessed that he was a business man. So distinguished was his bearing and character that one might have imagined him a high government official, a representative of aristocratic officialdom. He spoke little, but one had the impression that he took a lively interest in social conversations. In all his movements he was measured and calm, acting always with complete decorum. But behind this proud and worthy bearing the keen observer might have recognized a constant tiredness, a weariness that could not be concealed. At that time (1899) death was already nestling in the most important engine of the body. His heart would sometimes let him down. Conrad Berg was not one to admit defeat. He would not take a rest, but worked on without a break as if there was nothing particu╱ lar the matter with him, and simply accepted the risk.'

About Alban's mother, Watznauer writes: 'In matters of health Frau Johanna was the exact opposite of her husband. Robust and energetic, she found time to run—besides her own extensive household—a "devotional" shop (a shop dealing in cult objects in the Catholic religion) in the neighbourhood of the Stefanskirche. She could never understand how anybody could be ill. She could speak English and French well, was unusually well╱read, loved music and understood the artistic value of paintings and sculptures. She had the happy tempera╱ ment of the healthy, indigenous Viennese lass. Anything she set her hand to was sure to thrive; sentimentality and extrava╱ gant expressions of emotion were foreign to her nature. But under her rather rough exterior there was a warm and sensitive heart, and her goodness knew no bounds. However, should anyone have the unlucky idea of praising the good upbringing of her children, she would answer in a sharply defensive tone: "My children are not brought up at all!" She understood the word "upbringing" to mean something unnatural and to represent some sort of deformation, and this she hated.'

Besides Alban she bore three children: Alban's oldest brother Hermann was thirteen years his senior; he emigrated to America at an early age and attained a respectable position in business. Charley was three years his senior; this brother helped in his mother's shop and after his father's death managed an export firm of his own, modelled on his father's. Then came Smaragda, two years his junior; Alban and his sister, being in the same age-group, were particularly close friends as children. Of Alban himself, Watznauer writes: 'He was just under fourteen years old when I met him early in 1899. In the first classes of the secondary school he was an excellent schoolboy, but now—in the fourth class—he began to have difficulties. In childhood he had been what the Viennese call "a sturdy lad" —chubby and rather plump. At thirteen he had begun to shoot up; he was then too thin, and his days of rude good health were over. Yet he was a fine straightforward boy with a rascally face and two big, bright eyes casting sharp glances at the world around him. In his mental capacity he was far superior to his schoolfellows of the same age. Not that he knew more—he was not a precocious child, not a prodigy—he simply had a faculty for recognizing and evaluating quite ordinary things. Perhaps he developed this careful feeling for worth and worthlessness in the great packing rooms of his father's business and in his mother's warehouse. The accuracy of his judgment of works of art was already highly developed at that time. Musically, he could boast no special accomplishment. He took piano lessons from his sister's governess, but did not exhibit any great gift for the instrument.'

Life in the large parental apartment was generally happy. The highlights were provided by ambitious productions arranged by the old governess for the children to perform in front of the parents and their guests (declamatory and musical perfor-mances, *tableaux* and masquerades). Alban Berg's enjoyment of masquerade and all sorts of burlesque, which he showed again and again in later life, may well be attributed to these occasions.

In the spring of 1899 the family moved to the seventh *Bezirk* (Vienna VII, Breitegasse 8) because the Tuchlauben house was to be pulled down. In the autumn of this year Alban began to show a stronger preference for music; his interest was prob-ably aroused by his sister's excellent piano playing and the beautiful singing of his brother Charley. He played the piano with enthusiasm and wanted to communicate his joy in music to all the world around him. His interest in everything musical increased so vastly that his thirst for knowledge could hardly be quenched. On his fifteenth birthday Watznauer gave him 'The Golden Book of Music', a thick collection very popular in those days, which he studied avidly—twenty-five years later he found room to mention the book in an article.

On 30th March 1900 his father died suddenly of a heart attack. His business passed into the hands of strangers, and the family's financial affairs took a turn for the worse. The brother in America wanted Alban to come out to join him, but a well-off aunt offered to pay for his further studies, thus making it possible for him to stay at home.

His love for music increased still more in the next school year (1900–1). A performance of *Fidelio* at the opera made an enormous impression on him. Then came his first attempts at composition, completely self-taught: three songs, 'Heilige Himmel' (text by Franz Evers), 'Herbstgefühl' (Siegfried Fleischer), 'Minnelied' (Walther von der Vogelweide). His brothers and sisters sang these and many of the following songs over and over. The whole family took great pleasure in them, but nobody thought for a moment that music would ever be Alban's profession. This is not the place to speak of these songs in more detail, since the mature artist later rejected most of them. The choice of texts shows discrimination, and the songs grew from the best models (Schubert, Schumann, Brahms, Hugo Wolf). They strike a note of their own, and exceptional talent is visible in almost every bar.

Besides music, literature fascinated Alban at this stage. Testimony of his extraordinarily wide reading is given by the many quotations in his long epistolary discussions with Watznauer (letters of twenty pages and more!). The following excerpt from a letter of 20th November 1902 is characteristic of the high romantic spiritual state and style of the seventeen-year-old youth cultivating his 'beautiful pain': 'My dear

Hermann, you left us on Thursday . . . melancholy—as is un⁄
fortunately always the case with me—followed on the heels of
gaiety!! I was attacked again by that old life⁄pain, which clings
to me like some old inherited ill. I had a little to do—it was
soon done—and then I felt the tug of the piano. I wanted to
hold on to the first impression awakened in me by that poem of
Hoffmansthal's: "Hörtest du denn nicht hinein, dass Musik
das Haus durchdrang" . . . I got that far—but could not get
any further—then I read a little in "Poesy and Truth"—but it
gave me hardly any pleasure!— At last it was evening. Then,
to the suffering of my soul was added a physical pain; but it
was still such as I consider a beautiful pain. We dined. Then
a little more music: Grieg's magnificent Autumn Overture—
just right for my mood—then many beautiful things from
"Dalibor". We went to bed. I lay there with a heavy heart—
I had that feeling, when one clutches at one's oppressed heart
and wants only to plead: "Oh, please let it go slower—quite
quiet and gentle—be still!"—and thus I went to sleep, in the
happy conviction: for ever——' (At the end of the letter,
already overflowing with exclamation marks and dashes, there
is a big black cross—as was his custom at this time.)

Only a few days after his seventeenth birthday Alban was
shaken by the death of Hugo Wolf. The friends went to the
burial (24th February 1902). After his return from the church
Alban fell victim to a high fever. He wrote a few more songs
and duets that spring, and completely bound up in music and
literature as he was, the threat of the matriculation examinations
at school found him rather unprepared. He failed straight
away in the written examination; his German composition
was described as 'insufficient'. The reader may judge for him⁄
self to what extent this classification was justified—the follow⁄
ing is an excerpt from a twenty⁄eight⁄page letter sent to
Watznauer on 16th July 1903:

'So you call my fiasco in school a "joke on the part of fate"?!
—Far from seeing it in such a humorous light, I feel like
weeping when I think of it—, it is a drama with the saddest

kind of end—a tragedy—more tragic than many tragedies!!!—
How beautiful this summer would have been!—Liberty! magnificent liberty!!! golden felicity!—I believe I would have been
like a little child, wild with joy and delight!—Think of the joy
of living—the joy of working—they're the same after all!—But
now!?!—I'm too dull even for the joy of dying—joyless—I lack
the great joy—I even lack the great suffering!!?—It could be
so!—So I am a tentative seeker! Finding nothing! . . .'

It is worth emphasizing that this and most of the following
excerpts from letters are not to be considered as polished literary
exercises. They nevertheless show extraordinary strength of feeling and expression, and a sense of form that is to be manifested
in overwhelming fullness and variety in the musical compositions of the artist's maturity.

The gloom which followed the 'fiasco in school' was further
intensified in the next few months by a love affair which cul-
minated in a suicide attempt in the autumn of 1903. Even after
this crisis, the atmosphere of gloom persisted during the repetition of the highest class in secondary school (1903–4), and found
its musical expression in a few profoundly melancholy songs.
Berg said later that it was a complete mystery how he finally
managed to matriculate at all. But matriculate he did, and
enjoyed the summer of 1904 to his heart's content in the
'Berghof' on the shores of the Ossiachersee, free at last from
scholastic worries. The 'Berghof' was a modest farmhouse in
Kärnten, bought by his father and converted into a comfortable
summer residence. It remained the property of the family until
1919, and even after that Berg would often spend his 'working
holidays' there as a paying guest. The 'Berghof' and its sur-
roundings, in fact the lake landscape of Kärnten in general,
played a large part in Berg's life and work.

The following is a mood-picture from his first 'school-free'
summer in Kärnten (taken from letters to Watznauer of 1st and
20th August 1904): 'I am sitting alone in my room—father's
bust in front of me in the corner—further on my favourite
picture of Beethoven, then the statue of Brahms—to the left

and right of that, portraits of Mahler and Ibsen, my living
ideals. On my night table there is Beethoven again—a statue—
and over him my favourite painting (only a reproduction unfortunately): "Jupiter and Jo" by Correggio. There—that is
my surrounding—a little child of man set amongst gods and
heroes! . . . And now for a brief survey of my life here: the first
couple of days definitely doing nothing: industriously swimming, once a day so far—once even twice (the second swim was
at 7 in the evening in storm and rain—it was splendid!) face
and hands are getting brown,—eating and drinking (beer).
Proceeded with Goethe's letters to Frau von Stein. Studied
modern German lyric poetry (which is quite entertaining) . . .'
    '. . . Your description of the country and people was very
graphic—I could feel with you the longing for the highest
peaks of the snow mountains, for the clearest icy air—there
where one has the feeling that never could a lie cross your
lips . . . There were eight of us at dinner—it was very dark
round about, only here and there uncannily bright; for bright,
flashing lightning cleft the cloudy sky and bathed the lake in
garish blue. The foliage around us rustled weirdly—and our
lamps were like flares in a storm; lightning flashed over the
landscape again, like a glowing whip. In the distance a peal
of thunder, and a red glow crept up behind the mountains and
climbed—and grew, up into the clouds, that shone hideously
and threw down their purple glow to be reflected in the lake.
Then again lightning flashed across the night—the redness
disappeared for a moment as if vanquished by the lightning's
ray, and one could see yellowish-brown columns of smoke
climbing accusingly into the sky. Then red again—now
weaker, now more intense—and then it got darker and darker.
Just a faint glow on the bulging clouds—a dead grey on the
lake. The fires of victory leapt up now and again like the sound
of fading fanfares, until the battlefield lay empty and devastated.
The following day the careful housewife telegraphed to Vienna
"Charley, don't forget the fire insurance!"—' (The style and
punctuation of these letters is considerably influenced by the

writing of Peter Altenberg, a Viennese poet greatly admired by Alban.)

In October 1904 he entered the local government office (the highest administrative authority in the crown-land of lower Austria) as an unpaid accountant, and was supposed to set out on the respected and well-paid career of a civil servant—above all, this was in accordance with the wishes of his mother. Watznauer has given me a graphic description of the mean hole that Berg had to work in: his first business was to do with the statistics of the acquisition and disposal of pigs; later he dealt with the taxes on alcohol and distilleries. His office work, to which he applied himself dutifully but with no ambition whatever, soon pales into insignificance in the face of a decisive event which was to give the whole course of his life its final direction.

Arnold Schönberg had come to the attention of Charley Berg by way of an advertisement; he was living in Vienna and earning his living by teaching musical theory and composition. Charley secretly took some of his brother's songs under his arm and went to Schönberg. After looking through the compositions Schönberg invited Alban to come to him, and accepted the self-taught young man as his pupil. At first the lessons were free; he only began to accept a fee towards the end of 1905 when the finances of the Berg family took a turn for the better.

What Schönberg was able to give to his pupils in the way of artistic instruction, and what he meant to them as a human being, is manifested in the numerous publications in which his pupils give voice to their gratitude and respect for the beloved teacher. However, his pupils' active work bears witness more eloquent than any words to the greatness of the teacher, and Alban Berg, with Anton Webern, ranks among the highest of his pupils. Berg's whole artistic being was moulded by Schönberg in the most important way. It will be seen over and over again in this book how completely conscious Berg was of this fact, and how he acknowledged it frankly and gratefully his whole life long.

Berg made rapid progress under Schönberg's direction, not only in music but in his whole spiritual development. He worked with inflexible industry, relentlessly harnessing all his strength to his work. The great teacher's instruction brought him the greatest happiness, which was reflected in his whole appearance and in everything he did (as all agree who knew him at that time). Now with increased enthusiasm he went to concerts and the performances at the opera. Gustav Mahler, who inspired in Berg the most glowing admiration, was direc/ tor of the opera as a creative and interpretative artist. (As early as 1902, after the Viennese première of Mahler's Fourth Sym/ phony, Berg with a flock of young enthusiasts had stormed the artist's room and possessed himself of Mahler's bâton, which he preserved as a precious relic.)

The next years are filled with intensive studies with Schön/ berg. Besides systematic solutions of the exercises in musical theory, Berg brings the master his own attempts at composition and discusses them with him. In the summer of 1905 he wrote the first song that he was still to consider acceptable in later years: 'Im Zimmer', with text by Johannes Schlaf (*Seven Early Songs*, No. 5). At this time Berg was also playing a lot of orchestral music arranged for piano duet with his sister Smaragda, whom he also accompanied in her singing (once even in a pub/ lic concert). In the winter of 1905 he wrote 'Die Nachtigall' to words by Theodor Storm (*Seven Early Songs*, No. 3).

At the end of 1905 the family moved out into Hietzing, a residential suburb of Vienna. Shortly afterwards a legacy brought increased prosperity. The management of the inherited houses, delegated to Alban, was often to prove very trouble/ some, and weighed him down almost all his life.

The twenty/one/year/old Berg spent all his free time in unremitting musical work in a little gardenhouse that belonged to the family. He kept the blinds constantly closed so as not to be disturbed by the changing times of day. He fought his tiredness with excessive draughts of tea, a stimulant to which he often had recourse later in life.

The Austrian première of Richard Strauss's *Salome* in the opera house in Graz formed an interesting interruption in this wild burst of work. (Graz was chosen for the performance because the work could not be given in Vienna on account of its 'scandalous' text.) Berg made the journey with his friend Watznauer on 16th May 1906. Mahler, Zemlinsky, Schönberg and other progressive-minded Viennese musicians were also present at this memorable première.

This constant and intensive 'spare time' work began to damage Berg's health. In June 1906 he obtained sick leave from the office and went to the Berghof, where he continued to compose with his usual intensity. After resisting for a long time, his mother eventually agreed to his giving up his official post—in August he had received his definitive appointment— and devoting himself entirely to composition. Just before he left the office (end of October 1906) he was still struggling through a pile of work, and he wrote off all back tax due from the poor farmers as 'irrecoverable'.

In this season (1906–7)—the first in which Berg could take part as a 'free-lance artist'—the most important musical experiences were three concerts with works by Schönberg (Songs, 'Verklärte Nacht', Chamber Symphony and First String Quartet). Frequently in these concerts there was loud opposition from the audience; Berg answered these attacks with violent anger. Then there was the première of Mahler's Sixth Symphony, and the end of that great man's work in the Vienna Opera; there was also a visit from the Breslau opera company, who gave *Salome* in a Viennese theatre (Berg heard the work six times). He had also joined an amateur chorus directed by Schönberg (in which he sang bass). Of his compositions at this time 'Traumgekrönt', text by Rilke (*Seven Early Songs*, No. 4), and the beginning of the Piano Sonata, Opus 1, are worthy of mention.

In the opera house that winter Alban caught several glimpses of Helene Nahowski, who was later to become his wife. She too lived in Hietzing and was training to become an opera singer. He became acquainted with her personally at Easter 1907. The relationship grew closer and closer in the course of many visits to the opera and walks together.

A few of Berg's letters of this time have survived, and they show very clearly the point he had reached in his artistic development. Their 'matter-of-factness' is also highly remarkable, in contrast to the 'romantic' outpourings of the letters to Watznauer. The letters are addressed to a young girl—the daughter of an American business friend of Alban's father—who had spent the summers of 1903 and 1904 as a guest in the Berghof. For the most part the letters consist of enthusiastic descriptions of Gustav Mahler's work. The following passages are of general significance.

End of July 1907: '. . . This year I completed my counterpoint studies with Schönberg, and am very happy to have earned his approval (as I found out by chance). Now, next autumn, comes "composition". This summer I am to work hard, partly composing out of the blue (I am making a piano sonata for my own benefit like this) and partly repeating the counterpoint (6- to 8-part choruses and a fugue with two themes for string quintet and piano accompaniment). Naturally, I enjoy it all very much—and that's necessary; if I didn't enjoy it I'd never be able to do it! And of course Schönberg's enormous ability gives one a grandiose panoramic view of the whole literature of music, and a healthy and accurate judgment besides. And that's *good*! For our taste is all too easily corrupted by all the music that's simply flung together these days—and then highly praised by newspapers and public. Something really good is acknowledged only later on—if it happens early it's mostly just a matter of fashion! The masses have now arrived at R. Wagner—he deserves it!! They only respect the earlier masters—Bach, Beethoven, Mozart—because it would be a scandal if they didn't. But I wouldn't like to look into the souls of these people who applaud a Bach concerto, a late Beethoven quartet or even a Mozart aria or minuet with such enthusiasm, for fear of seeing the deadly boredom there.

This situation is most clearly apparent in the public's under/
standing—or rather, misunderstanding—of Brahms, who in
his way—Lieder, piano music, chamber music, even the sym/
phonies and masses, etc.—did things at least as great as what
Wagner did in opera, and yet he seemed unspeakably boring
to the public and now shares the fate of Beethoven, Bach,
Schubert, etc. i.e. one *acts* enthusiastic!!! Well, ten years ago
Richard Strauss coined the phrase about the "bogged (philis/
tine) Wagnerians" whom he regards as the most dangerous
enemies of music, more dangerous even than the race of people
who always send the old classics into the breach. For those are
the ones who always say when they hear something new:
"We Wagnerians, we are certainly up/to/date, nobody can say
we hang onto the Old (it was we, after all, who introduced
even Hugo Wolf and Bruckner to the public and made them
comprehensible) . . ." And then it's easy after such a beauti/
fully prepared premise to deal a clever blow to anything really
modern, really *new*, however great and significant it may be.
And the public falls for it—they fall for it gladly because they
are just as ignorant and philistine as the pen/pushers who have
just arrived at Wagner—pen/pushers for the newspapers or
pen/pushers on music paper, it is all the same!! . . .'

And on 18th November 1907: '. . . and now for literature:
Wedekind—the really new direction—the emphasis on the
sensual in modern works!! You have sharp eyes, dear Miss
Frida! This trait is at work in all new art. And I believe it is a
good thing. At last we have come to the realization that
sensuality is not a weakness, does not mean a surrender to one's
own will. Rather is it an immense strength that lies in us—the
pivot of all being and thinking. (Yes; all thinking!) In this I
am declaring firmly and certainly the great importance of
sensuality, for everything spiritual. Only through the under/
standing of sensuality, only through a fundamental insight
into the "depths of mankind" (shouldn't it rather be called
the "heights of mankind"?) can one arrive at a real idea of the
human psyche. This achievement, mastered first by Medicine

and Psychology understandably enough, is now making its way slowly into Jurisprudence, God be praised, and there it will produce the most wonderful fruits for humanity (I need only mention two names: Lombroso and Krafft-Ebing). But from earliest times it has always been the case that that which the whole world has assimilated only gradually was *inborn* in the great spiritual heroes, the geniuses of the world. And now I could list you a whole herd of names and you would immediately remember how significant—yes, and often decisive—was the rôle played by sensuality in their creations. Homer! How he traces back all action, even that of the gods—i.e. the most spiritual characters—to their sensual feelings, often of the most primitive sort! And is Shakespeare any different?? Isn't he the greatest knower of men and therefore the greatest poet?! And Goethe must be mentioned!!! Why then shouldn't we, the newer ones—who have at last arrived at consciousness of what the great men of old only realized instinctively—why shouldn't we hold fast to this great knowledge?!! That's why men like Strindberg and Wedekind are great psychologists—knowers of men in the truest sense of the word. Whether they are also great poets, that is a matter that posterity will have to decide; *I* believe it . . .'

And from the same letter some remarks that are very characteristic of Berg's creative nature: '. . . If possible, I have become even more shy of men and even less capable of taking a leading position in life. I only feel happy when I can quietly pursue my life of work, untouched by the noise and bustle of the outside world. Only then can I find the possibility and delight of writing. Only then can I find satisfaction and a supportable life! That's why the recent concert in which, as you will see from the enclosed programme, some things of mine were included, make an impression more painful than pleasing on my sensibilities, despite the fact that I enjoyed a certain success. I can say frankly that my fugue was the most successful piece of the evening, although things were performed that were on a much higher plane. That's the public for you! I could see it best in the case of my three songs. The best one (from 'Traum⁄ gekrönt') did not please anyone—the crowd was enthusiastic about the weakest one ('Nachtigall'). So you will not be sur⁄ prised, Miss Frida, that I have no respect whatever for the "crowd" and am happy when I can keep out of their way.'

The concert mentioned in the letter represents Berg's first public appearance as a composer. It was an evening devoted to compositions by Schönberg's pupils in the Saal des Gremiums of the Wiener Kaufmannschaft on 7th November 1907. Berg was represented in the programme with three songs ('Liebesode', 'Die Nachtigall', 'Traumgekrönt', sung by Elsa Pazeller, ac⁄ companied by Karl Horwitz) and a Double Fugue for String Quintet with Piano Accompaniment (after the Manner of a Continuo) in which he himself played the piano part. On the same evening works by Horwitz, Ivanow, Jalowetz, Webern, Weyrich, Stein and Wilma von Webenan were also performed. The audience included Alma Maria Mahler and Alexander Zemlinsky. The only traceable review (in the *Neuen Wiener Journal*) runs as follows: 'Eight different talents—what they have in common is the rare seriousness of their aspirations. All mat⁄ ters to do with the craft of compositional technique, rules of harmony, polyphonic voice⁄leading are handled with impres⁄ sive sureness, and by some with real virtuosity. The sense for the character of sound⁄effects is always on the alert; in some composers one notices a remarkable talent for the logical con⁄ struction of forms. There is conspicuous resistance against light⁄fingered effects. The valuable results of good training are respect for art, purity of feeling, sureness of style. It is wonderful how Schönberg's powerful and original personality guides the talents of these pupils strongly and surely in this way.' Never again has such a favourable and understanding judgment been expressed by an outsider on the subject of Schönberg's teaching in Vienna.

In the autumn of 1907 Gustav Mahler's work in Vienna came to an end. Paul Stefan has given a lively description of the details of his farewell in his chronicle 'Das Grab in Wien'

1   Berg's grandfather, Joseph Berg (1791–?)

2   His father, Conrad Berg (1846–1900)

3   His mother, Johanna Berg, née Braun (1851–1926)

In diesem Haus hier geboren — und doch nicht bodenständig...

4   Berg's birthplace, Vienna I, Tuchlauben 8

(1913): 'Mahler, accompanied by his wife, began his trip to America on 9th December. Shortly beforehand it had been noised abroad that the loyal might be with him at the last moment and see him off at the station. When we finally dis-covered the date of his departure, some friends distributed a short note: "The admirers of Gustav Mahler will meet to take their farewells of him on Monday, 9th December before 8.30 a.m. on the platform at the Westbahnhof, and they invite you to appear there, and also to inform any friends who are of the same persuasion. Since Mahler is to be surprised by this demonstration it is urgently requested that anyone having any-thing to do with the Press should not be taken into your confidence." Whoever witnessed the greetings of those who came (there were about two hundred), whoever saw how heartily and effusively each one pressed Mahler's hand, how friendly and pleased he was to return the pressure, whoever heard him—usually so sparing with words—speak in such a friendly manner to these faithful followers,—whoever saw all this could not have found it in his heart to grudge him—or rather all the others—this last pleasure. Everything had been arranged overnight, and no "official" personalities had been informed. There was no admixture of artificiality; we all had only one urgent desire in our hearts: to see him again, the man to whom we owed so much ... The train moved. And a remark of Gustav Klimt's expressed what we were all fearfully feeling about such a great time: "It's over!" ...' It was in this hour of farewell that Berg was for the first time in a position to speak to Mahler personally. Gustav Klimt also meant a great deal to him. He retained his high opinion of Klimt's painting all his life.

In the spring of 1908 Berg had two striking theatrical experiences: Wedekind's *Frühlings Erwachen* in the German Volkstheater, and *Ariadne and Bluebeard* by Paul Dukas in the Volksoper. The Dukas work impressed Berg particularly; in it he saw for the first time the use of variation form for musico-dramatic purposes, a procedure that was later to achieve such great significance in his two operas, as is well known. His compositions at this time included Nos. 1 and 2 of the *Early Songs*: 'Nacht' (text by Carl Hauptmann) and 'Schilflied' (Lenau). In the summer he completed the Piano Sonata, Opus 1 at the Berghof. He also sketched the *Four Songs* to poems by Hebbel and Mombert, Opus 2, at this time.

But his creative happiness was marred by severe physical and mental suffering. At the age of twenty-three (on 23rd July) he had his first attack of bronchial asthma, a sickness that was to plague him often and rob him of the peace necessary for work. He was examined by Sigmund Freud who was spending the summer on the Ossiachersee, and the latter's personality made a tremendous impression on him. Berg dated his fateful relationship to the number 23—which was to have significance for him so often in his life—from the day (23rd July) of his first attack. In general he was disposed to regard all the physical ills that pursued him as resulting from spiritual upsets. In this view, which he repeated again and again in later years both in conversation and correspondence, he was following a theory of Schönberg's; Schönberg was his absolute authority not only in art but in all things.

At that time it can truly be said that there was no lack of spiritual upsets: his desire to make Helene Nahowski his wife as soon as possible met with resistance from her parents. They considered marriage ill-advised on account of the labile state of Alban's health. Many passages in his letters to his betrothed bear witness to the pain caused him by this uncertainty. Two sentences from a letter written in the summer of 1908 must suffice as evidence of this: 'But no word about my pain, my fear, my longing for deliverance! I shall wait and wait—perhaps some unexpected line from you will deliver me from my fear— let it be said: my fear of losing you—'. The suffering that Helene Nahowski had to bear is reflected in three sketches dedicated to her by Peter Altenberg ('H.N.', 'Bekanntschaft', and 'Besuch im einsamen Park'). The poet included these in the book he published in 1911, *Neues Altes*. Alban too figures in 'Bekanntschaft'; at this period he often visited the poet, who held him in great affection.

As consolation for these personal troubles, his intensive musical work progresses by strides. Schönberg's pupils pre/ pared another concert of their own works, this time on a larger scale. On 18th November 1908 they hired the large hall of the Musikverein and engaged a professional orchestra for half the concert. Anton Webern's Passacaglia, Opus 1 was given its first performance, under the composer's bâton, and Berg's Twelve Variations on an Original Theme for piano were also on the programme (played by Irene Bien). The following reviews of this work have survived: 'After only eight bars the variations got tangled up in a maze of indescribable modula/ tions'. 'No theme, but twelve variations on it.' 'Berg's Varia/ tions, fine and rich in melodic invention, excellently written for the instrument, show a strong talent for composition. Techni/ cally, he has obviously learnt a lot from Brahms.'

The reference to Brahms is completely justified: the variations are not so much an independent creative achievement of Berg's; they are, rather, a striking example of the strict discipline im/ posed on himself by this young and imaginative artist while he was a pupil of Schönberg's. This discipline is much more in evidence in this 'student work' than in the songs written at about the same time. It was just this discipline that increased his value in his master's eyes, and from now on Schönberg discusses his own creative projects with Berg much more openly. Many of Berg's remarks at this time bear witness to the happiness occasioned by such trust.

First Interlude

'Two things emerged clearly even from Berg's earliest compositions, however awkward they may have been: first, that music was to him a language, and that he really expressed himself in that language; and secondly: overflowing warmth of feeling. He was eighteen at the time—that is a long while ago and I cannot say if I recognized originality even at that stage. It was a pleasure to teach him. He was industrious, eager, and did everything in the best possible way. And—like all those young people of that time—he was soaked in music, lived in music. He went to all operas and concerts and knew all the music; at home he played piano duets and was soon reading scores. He was enthusiastic and uncritical, receptive to the beautiful whether old or new, whether music, literature, painting, sculpture, theatre or opera.

'I could do countpoint with him in a manner rare amongst my pupils. And I would like to mention a fivepart double fugue for string quintet that was overflowing with ingeniosities. But I could see already to what lengths he could be pushed: when the fugue was ready I told him to add a piano accompaniment in the manner of a continuo. Not only did he execute this with all excellence, he found ways of adding a further host of minor devilries.

'The instruction in composition that followed proceeded effortlessly and smoothly up to and including the Sonata. Then problems began to appear, the nature of which neither of us understood then. I know it today: obviously Alban, who had occupied himself extraordinarily intensively with contemporary music, with Mahler, Strauss, perhaps even Debussy whose work I did not know, but certainly with my music—it is sure that Alban had a burning desire to express himself no longer in the classical forms, harmonies, and melodic forms and their proper schemata of accompaniment, but in a manner in ac' cordance with the times, and with his own personality which had been developing in the meantime. A hitch was apparent in his creative activity.

'I cannot remember what he worked on with me afterwards. Others can report more reliably on this point. One thing is sure: his String Quartet (Opus 3) surprised me in the most unbelievable way by the fullness and unconstraint of its musical language, the strength and sureness of its presentation, its careful working and significant originality.

'That was the time when I moved to Berlin (1911) and he was left to his own devices. He has shown that he was equal to the task.

'For some time we only saw each other relatively rarely, for at that time Berg had a horror of travelling. He only overcame this much later, but then completely.

'Unshakable conscientiousness and reliability were very characteristic of Berg. Whatever he undertook he executed with painful exactitude—thought it through from the ground up and then corrected and proofed it carefully. From this one can easily estimate the value of his work for our "Verein für musikalische Privataufführungen" (Society for Private Per' formances).

'And then he was the truest and most affectionate of friends. His power of invention was inexhaustible when it was a matter of preparing a pleasant surprise for someone; it was on the same plane as the intensity of his composing. And this bears out something which I said about myself and which applies perhaps to anyone who is really working at himself. I said: "Whether I am composing, painting, teaching, book' binding, rowing, swimming . . . it is all the same. I have to do all these things with the same amount of fervour! The same is true of Berg and of Webern, and it is probably this that binds us together,—this is probably the reason we are so close to one another."

'I wish I had the time to speak exhaustively of his work as well. Most of it I know only from the scores. In recent years I have heard (besides the first works) *Wozzeck*, the Lyric Suite, the Chamber Concerto, and—on a very imperfect gramophone record—the Violin Concerto. Of this last I would just like to say that it is reminiscent of his anxious facial expression when something had aroused his friendly sympathy. What an easy thing it was to call forth this sympathy! I always had the im⁄ pression that he had experienced beforehand what people close to him were going through, as though he had already suffered with them when they were suffering, so that when they came to tell him of it it did not catch him unawares but rather on the contrary reopened old wounds. Wounds that he had already inflicted on himself by his powerful sympathy. "Dem Anden⁄ ken eines Engels gewidmet"; dedicated to the memory of an angel. That child was an angel for him before she was an angel for others. For this angel was in him.'

ARNOLD SCHÖNBERG (1936)

LAST YEARS OF PEACE, AND THE
TIME OF THE FIRST WORLD WAR

The String Quartet, Opus 3, completed in the spring of 1910, was the last work of Berg's on which Schönberg had some direct influence. For a few more months Berg continued to visit the master twice a week for lessons, but these were occupied for the most part with discussing the piano score of Schönberg's *Gurrelieder* which Berg was engaged in making. They also analysed works by Gustav Mahler. 'Officially' the young composer's period of study was over; he had just had printed at his own expense his Opus 1 (Piano Sonata) and Opus 2 (*Four Songs*), for which he drew the title pages himself. But he kept the inexorable dominating personality of his master constantly before him, and humbly submitted everything he wrote in the first decade of his independence to Schönberg's strict judgment.

That same spring there occurred a last extended meeting with Mahler—at a larger gathering. The description which follows is based on Paul Stefan's chronicle 'Das Grab in Wien', but I have added the little episode about Webern—it was Berg who told me about this incident. Mahler came back from America and as usual spent a few weeks in Vienna. One evening he left his Döbling apartment to go to the nearby restaurant 'zum Schutzengel' and meet 'the young people'. Using Zemlinsky and Schönberg as his mouthpieces he had let it be known that he liked to spend time together with young people. They came, found him in a private room and listened. For Mahler talked, talked almost alone; the others hardly dared to throw in a word. It was not long before he came to speak of his beloved Dostoyevsky. But it was apparent that he was not really being understood, because hardly anybody knew Dostoyevsky's books in any detail. Mahler: 'You must change that, Schönberg! Have your pupils read Dostoyevsky, that is more important than counterpoint!' Silence. Then Webern raised his hand like a little boy in elementary school and said very timidly: 'Please, we've had Strindberg.' General laughter . . . Gradually the noise became too much for such a small room. Everyone went out. A couple of hangers-on took their departure, but the rest of us walked over the Hohe Warte and entered the 'Casino Zögernitz'. There too we quickly found a back room, and Mahler was again surrounded. He spoke enthusiastically of Schumann and told of his repeated efforts to get the symphonies to sound better by changing the instrumentation. But that could never have satisfied him . . . As we took our leave, he said, warding off admiring words about his work at the opera: 'Those were only experiments. The real thing still lies ahead. . .'

On 3rd May Berg attended a reading by the Viennese poet and satirist Karl Kraus (1874–1936) whose acquaintance he had made a year earlier through Peter Altenberg. As early as 1905 Berg had received a profound and lasting impression from the speech (*see p. 156*) made by Kraus at the première of Wedekind's *Buchse der Pandora*. Kraus himself had arranged to have the play put on. It was with reference to this speech that Berg dedicated a page from *Lulu* (Act II: 'Eine Seele die sich im Jenseits den Schlaf aus den Augen reibt . . .'—'A soul in Paradise rubbing the sleep from her eyes . . .') to Kraus on the occasion of his sixtieth birthday (28th April 1934). The dedication runs as follows: 'Permit me, honoured Mr Karl Kraus, to greet you on your sixtieth birthday as you will be celebrated on your hundredth birthday by the whole world— both the German speaking world and the Austrian thinking one. That is, as one of the greatest Austrian artists, as one of the greatest masters of German.'

The pleasure of reading 'Die Fackel' (torch, or flare), the paper founded by Kraus in 1899, accompanied Berg through-out his life. He was passionately involved in everything

ALBAN · BERG

VIER · LIEDER

FÜR · EINE · SINGSTIME
MIT · KLAVIER · OPUS · 2
NACH · GEDICHTEN · VON
HEBBEL · UND · MOMBERT

VERLAG · DER · SCHLESINGER'SCHEN
BUCH = UND · MUSIKHANDLUNG
BERLIN · (ROB. UND · WILH. LIENAU)
CARL · HASLINGER ᵍᵉᵐ TOBIAS WIEN
AUFFÜHRUNGS = UND · ALLE · ANDERN
RECHTE · VORBEHALTEN: PR. 2 MK.
„IN DIE UNIVERSAL-EDITION AUFGENOMMEN"
U. E. Nº 8813

pertaining to Kraus, though in later years they never met personally. Important aspects of Berg's view of the world stem
from Kraus, particularly his critical attitude to the culture of
his time, and Austrian culture especially. His carefully filed
literary style—capable of the clearest, most matter-of-fact presentation and the finest, sharpened polemics—was also decisively influenced by Kraus.

In the autumn of 1910 Berg met Mahler once on more
intimate terms; the memory was still very alive when he told
me about the occasion, twenty years later. It took place in the
home of Mahler's brother-in-law, the famous quartet leader
Arnold Rosé. Schönberg's String Quartet in F-sharp minor
was to be played for Mahler's benefit. At some point in the
evening Mahler asked the young composer if he were also a
conductor. Berg replied in the negative and Mahler said, 'Only
composing! That's the only right way.'

1911

24th April: premières of the Piano Sonata, Opus 1 and the
String Quartet, Opus 3 in a concert organized by the Viennese
Society for Art and Culture in the Ehrbarsaal. The performers
were the pianist Etta Werndorf and a string quartet brought
together *ad hoc* for the occasion. The only traceable review runs:
'Under the cloak and name of "String Quartet", this genre is
maltreated at the instigation of Mr Alban Berg. The same Mr
Berg has written a piano piece (boldly entitled "Piano Sonata")
which shows *traces* [spaced out in the original] of talent and
musicality.'

On 3rd May Berg married Helene Nahowski. Even the
man happy enough to have enjoyed the more intimate personal
acquaintance of the couple can only have a vague idea what this
woman came to mean to him. No one could completely grasp
what she meant to the *artist* Alban Berg no less than to the
man. Beyond her delightful relationship to the man, Helene not
only accompanied her husband on most of his journeys, but—
with her finely cultivated heart and spirit—became the critical

adviser of the composer in his work. Her presence gave the artist the peace and comfort of a relaxed home life, and the quiet necessary for undisturbed creative work. After Berg's death his widow was the most faithful guardian of his works, and created a lasting and meaningful memorial to him by setting up —with the revenue from his works—an 'Alban Berg Founda' tion' for the furthering of young composers.

The death of Gustav Mahler on 18th May was a very painful event for the young couple. Schönberg attended the burial with his pupils and dedicated his 'Harmonielehre'—which was just in the press—to the departed, and later celebrated him in a long memorial speech. Berg worked intensively on the correc' tions for this book. At the same time he undertook to make the piano score for Franz Schreker's opera *Der Ferne Klang* for Universal Edition, Vienna. The friendship with Schreker lasted throughout his life.

At this time, Berg's concern for Schönberg occupied his thoughts a great deal. Schönberg's finances had undergone a catastrophic turn for the worse; witness the following call sent out by Berg in September:

'Arnold Schönberg's friends and pupils consider it their duty to bring his extremity to the notice of the public. Shame prevents him from doing so himself; that is why we take the initiative and cry for help over his head. Our mouths are opened by the thought of this artist coming to grief for lack of the common necessities of life. Catastrophe has overtaken him with unexpected speed, and help from a distant source would be too late. For at the time of writing these lines, Schönberg is living, deprived of any means whatever, in a village near Munich. (The above call will be sent to patrons of the arts with a view to a monetary collection. You are requested to support the planned action by appending your signature. We urgently beg for your early reply to: Alban Berg, Vienna XIII, Trauttmannsdorffgasse 27.)'

This call brought in about forty signatures, but meanwhile the intended money collection had been invalidated, since

Schönberg's situation had improved with his move to Berlin. However, Berg intervened personally on Schönberg's behalf by approaching several influential people in Vienna, but with‐ out success. The address given at the end of the above call for help was the Bergs' first and only Viennese address. The artist's workroom has been left in exactly the condition it was in when Berg died. His widow still lives there. In 1961 the City of Vienna had a memorial plaque affixed to the outside wall.

Two important spiritual experiences took place towards the end of the year. The first was the première of Mahler's 'Lied von der Erde' on 20th November in Munich, conducted by Bruno Walter. Webern was also present, and the moving response to the occasion is documented in the letters he wrote to Berg. The second experience was a polemical lecture on 11th December by Adolf Loos (1870–1933), the architect friend of Karl Kraus and Peter Altenberg. The subject of the lecture was the house that Loos had built on the Michaeler‐ platz opposite the Wiener Hofburg; the undecorated façade was the subject of the most violent discussions in Vienna. As long as he lived, Loos remained Berg's warm and honoured friend.

1912

The beginning of the year was occupied with work on a book devoted to Schönberg; it was produced by his pupils and pub‐ lished by Piper‐Verlag, Munich. The book not only reviewed Schönberg's work as composer, theoretician and teacher, but also his activity as a painter (the contributors were Wassily Kandinsky and Paris von Gütersloh, and five paintings by Schönberg were reproduced. Berg wrote the final contribution, devoted 'To the teacher': 'From the very outset, Genius is instructive. His speech is a lesson, his activity is an example, his works are revelations. In him are the teacher, the prophet and the messiah; and the spirit of language—which knows better than the spirit of those who *maltreat* language how to

grasp the essence of genius—gives the creative artist the name
"master" and says about him that he "starts a school". The
realization of this alone would be sufficient to convince an
era of Arnold Schönberg's predestination to the office of
teacher,—that is if the era had any idea of the significance of
this artist and man. It is natural that an era has no idea of this,
for if it had the faculty of having an idea, of having a sense of
something that contradicts its nature—as does everything non-
temporal—then an era would not be the opposite of eternity.
And yet it is only on the premise of the realization that it is an
artist's vocation to teach, as a general proposition, that we can
arrive at a right judgment of Schönberg's way of teaching in
particular. This, the only justifiable way of teaching, insepar-
able from Schönberg's art and his significant humanity, is
further advanced by his explicit will to pursue the profession
of teacher. And this, like every great artistic will, whether
directed towards creative work, reproduction, criticism or
finally the profession of teaching, must of necessity call forth
the highest [from the pupils]. An exhaustive appraisal of this
miracle, born of such premises and conditions as these, would
imply a presumptuous attempt to solve the problem of genius
and fathom the secrets of the Divinity,—an attempt that would
inevitably come to grief on the impossibility of measuring the
immeasurable and setting limits to the limitless. Never can we
get beyond an attempt—an attempt which can be compared
with that of describing the beauty, richness and sublimity of the
waves of the sea. The happy swimmer, surrendered to the
unending currents, will be carried out on the highest waves
towards eternity, easily and proudly abandoning those who
are smashed to pieces on the rocks of their spiritual sterility,
and those who remain behind in the safe harbour of their
temporality.'

Many years later Berg told me he considered this text too
solemn and sophisticated. However, since it is very characteristic of his youthful excesses of feeling, and of his deep-
rooted admiration—which survived all the storms of life—for

Schönberg both as man and artist, it could not justifiably be omitted here.

In June great things came to pass in Vienna's musical life: the 'Wiener Musikfestwoche' was instituted and in it Bruno Walter conducted the première of Mahler's Ninth Symphony. This festival completely ignored the living composers, so the 'Akademische Verband für Literatur und Musik' organized a counter-festival with two evenings of contemporary music, and the programme included Berg's Piano Sonata. The programme book for these concerts also contained an article entitled 'Anton von Webern and Alban Berg' by their fellow pupil Karl Linke. The passage principally referring to Berg runs as follows: 'Whereas, in Webern, the complexes of feeling are concentrated inwards, in Berg they press stormily towards an outward resolution. Whereas in the former the factor of rest is presented in the emotion, in the latter the emotion, with all its build-ups, climaxes and subsidiary phenomena, is the object of the presentation. In the case of Berg, catastrophes of the soul are discharged outwards with elemental force. In his most misunderstood song (Opus 2, No. 4: 'Warm die Lüfte . . .') this becomes an event in nature: everything is aroused, wild and menacing, but moving towards deliverance and liberation. A dying-away such as occurs at the words "Das macht die Welt so tiefschön"—which at the same time introduces a new complex of feelings—shows most clearly the intensity of the calm after the storm. The sensibility of his feeling breaks out at the end after the removal of everything that had been a burden to it. The great events of the day had dulled the emotions; their pristine clarity had to be recreated by means of a process of purification. Every one of his pieces of music is a struggle for this purity.'

A letter to Webern written from the Berghof on the Ossia-chersee on 29th July contains a glowing tribute to Strindberg, occasioned by the dramas *Advent* and *Rausch*. He also points out the profound musicality that fills these dramas. At the end of the letter Berg announces his intention of moving in about two weeks to Trahütten in the Steiermark (a country property of his wife's family): 'I hope I'll do some work up there. At least finish the five orchestral songs! And afterwards in Vienna something big,—I feel it enormously urgent and compelling. If only my health holds!' The songs he mentions are the Five Orchestral Songs to Postcard Texts by Peter Altenberg, Opus 4. 'Something big' alludes to Berg's intention of writing a symphony or orchestral suite; he realized this intention two years later in his Three Pieces for Orchestra, Opus 6; the adagio of the planned symphony became the interlude before the last scene in the opera *Wozzeck*.

On Christmas Day Berg informs Webern—who was em⁄ployed as a theatre conductor in Stettin—that he is working on a thematic analysis of Schönberg's *Gurrelieder* (this was published by Universal Edition, Vienna in February 1913), and further that he is about to undertake a difficult task that is completely new to him: Franz Schreker had asked him to rehearse the choruses of the *Gurrelieder* ('So now I am study⁄ing the choruses, the parts and everything at a mad pace, and anticipate the first rehearsal with joy and trembling . . .').

1913
On 23rd February Franz Schreker directed the première of the *Gurrelieder* in Vienna. The work was a great success, and Schönberg, who had returned from Berlin and was present at most of the rehearsals, decided to conduct an orchestral concert. The programme is to include—besides Schönberg's Chamber Symphony, Opus 9, Orchestral songs by Zemlinsky and Mahler's 'Kindertotenlieder'—the premières of Webern's Six Pieces for Large Orchestra, Opus 6, and two of Berg's 'Altenberglieder' (Nos. 2 and 4). The concert was fixed for 31st March and was to take place in the large hall of the Musikverein as part of the general programme of the 'Aka⁄demische Verband für Literatur und Musik'. According to the report of one Viennese newspaper, the concert ended as follows: 'After Schönberg's Opus 9 the shrill sounds of rattling keys

and whistles was regrettably mixed up with the furious hissing and clapping, and the first brawl of the evening started in the second gallery. On all sides people were confusedly shrieking their opinions, and in the interval—abnormally long as it was—the opposing factions contrived to get in close to one another. But two Orchestral Songs on Postcard Texts by Peter Alten/berg, by Alban Berg, robbed even those who had soberly accepted the preceding works of their composure. The first poem runs: "Did you see the woods after the thunder/shower?!? Everything unbends, gleams and is more beautiful than before. Look here, woman, you too need a thunder/shower!" The music to these gaily nonsensical postcard texts exceeds everything that has been heard before, and it is to the credit of Viennese good/humouredness that the audience was ready merely to laugh heartily when they heard it. But excite/ment, confused quarrels, scrapping and insults broke out afresh when Schönberg stopped in the middle of a song and shouted at the audience that he would have every disturber of the peace taken out by the public authorities. Mr von Webern also cried out from his box that the whole baggage should be thrown out, and from the public came the answer that all the adherents of this odious direction in music should be taken away to the Steinhof lunatic asylum. The brawling and bawling in the hall continued without end. It was no rarity to see some gentlemen from the audience clambering over several rows of stalls in a breathless hurry and with ape/like agility—just for the sake of clouting the object of his rage. When the Com/missioner of Police finally stepped in there was nothing he could do in this chaos of wild, whipped/up passion. . . . Now all kinds of people stormed up on the musicians—who were pale with fright and shivering with excitement—and implored them to leave the stage. Even so it was probably half an hour before the last rowdies had left the hall.'

The only remark of Berg's that has come to my notice on the subject of this historic scandal—which was followed, inci/dentally, by legal proceedings—is a sentence contained in a

5 Schoolboy in the second class

6   Berg at the age of twenty

7 June 1908

8 Demobbed from the First Regiment of Infantry at the end of 1916

letter to Webern: 'The whole thing is so loathsome that one would like to fly far away.'

Berg's visit to Schönberg in Berlin at the beginning of June can probably be understood as a sort of 'flight' in a higher sense. The beginning of this meeting was very pleasurable. Berg wrote enthusiastically to Webern on 6th June and was pleased above all by a full rehearsal of the melodrama cycle 'Pierrot Lunaire' (which had been completed and premièred in the autumn of 1912) arranged by Schönberg especially for his benefit. The experience of this rehearsal was uncommonly strong and lasting. More than a year later—on 20th July 1914 —he wrote to Schönberg on the subject: '. . . All I know is that the two times I heard Pierrot it made the deepest impres-sion on me that I have ever received from a work of art; the puzzling force of these pieces has left indelible marks on my insides.'

But on his last day in Berlin Berg had an argument with Schönberg which profoundly upset him. It seems that Schön-berg pointed out in no uncertain terms various weaknesses that he found in the current work of his one-time pupil. It must have been the aphoristic form of the latest pieces—the Altenberg songs and the Four Pieces for Clarinet and Piano, Opus 5, completed in the spring of 1913—that occasioned Schönberg's vehement censure; they were so brief as to exclude any possibility of extended thematic development. There is something deeply moving about the manner in which Berg accepted this censure, particularly when one reads the following lines written to Schönberg on 14th June, directly after his return to Vienna: 'But I must thank you for your censure just as much as for everything you ever gave me, in the full know-ledge that it is meant well—and for my own good. I need not tell you, my dear Mr Schönberg, that the great pain it caused me is a guarantee that I have taken your criticism to heart. And if I succeed in my good resolution, this pain too will have lost its bitterness and will become one of those memories which —as always when you spoke to my conscience with implacable truth—despite their depressing side are full of profound, though serious beauty.'

After his return from Berlin, Berg began work at Trahütten in the summer on a large orchestral piece which he intended to dedicate to Schönberg on the latter's fortieth birthday (9th September 1914), and which he also hoped would prove the fulfilment of the good resolution brought about by Schönberg's criticism. To start with he was thinking of a 'gay suite', but it turned into the Three Orchestral Pieces, Opus 6, and about two years were necessary for their completion.

1914–1918

In May 1914 Berg went to several performances of Büchner's drama fragment *Woyzeck* (with Albert Steinrück in the title rôle) at the Vienna Chamber Theatre; shortly afterwards he decided to make the work into an opera. Work on the arrange‑ ment of the text ran alongside the composition of the orchestral pieces. On 8th September he sent a fair copy of the score of Nos. 1 and 3 (Präludium and March) to Schönberg as a birthday present, and in the accompanying letter he gives the master a detailed description of the second piece, though Schönberg had to wait until August 1915 to receive the fair copy of the score of this. Berg introduces a motif from the March in the second and third scenes of the first act of *Wozzeck* (*see p.* 126).

The Great War broke out in August 1914. In the first months of the war one of Berg's chief worries was the fate of Schönberg; he was intensely concerned about the latter's poor financial situation, as well as about his periods of military service (December 1915 to September 1916, and July to October 1917). Berg himself had to join the army in the middle of August 1915 (First Regiment of Infantry, Vienna). After two months he was sent to the school for reserve officers in Bruck an der Leitha, or rather in the neighbouring Hungarian village of Kiralyhida. There he had to survive a real period of suffering; a year after his death a Viennese newspaper (*Der*

Wiener Tag of 25th December 1946) printed a graphic account of it, and what follows is for the most part a literal transcription:
    Service in the officer's training school was a great strain. The field exercises with full marching equipment, and the forma﹍tion of battle lines—the soldiers constantly throwing them﹍selves to the ground and springing up again—these exercises in particular far exceeded Berg's strength. Bad catarrh, shortage of breath, heavy attacks of asthma were the results of his exertions; but in spite of his exhaustion he could hardly sleep. On one occasion, when his pupil Gottfried Kassowitz visited him at the Karalyhida barracks, he spoke about his sleepless nights: 'Have you ever heard a lot of people all snoring at the same time? The polyphonic breathing, gasping and groaning makes the strangest chorus I have ever heard. It is like a music of the primeval sounds that rises from the abysses of these people's souls.' Reading this, it is impossible not to think of the barracks scene at the end of the second act of *Wozzeck*, where—the curtain is still closed—the snoring chorus of sleep﹍ing soldiers enters 'like a sound of nature'.

In November he suffered a complete physical breakdown. Private (such was the rank to which he had been promoted) Alban Berg was taken to the hospital for examination, and the report was: 'Bronchial asthma. Inflation of the lungs. Lobes of the lung more than a handsbreadth. Breathing rough . . .' At the beginning of December Berg was detailed to sentry duty in Vienna. Here too he suffered treatment very similar to the experiences of the tormented soldier Wozzeck. As evidence we have the following drastic passages from a letter written to Kassowitz on Christmas day 1915: 'Some﹍where there is a law to the effect that volunteers of one year's standing (matriculated) cannot be used for guard duty, only for office work. My being detailed to guard duty is simply an injustice, made even more crass by the fact that perfectly ordi﹍nary guards are placed in offices simply by means of a little protection—and there they sit, and even rise month by month! Apart from this, the guard duty is such that my health has again deteriorated and will continue to do so. It is furthermore impossible for me to get the proper medical treatment, since more attention is paid to flat feet and broken limbs, etc. than to internal illnesses. And my illness is of such a kind that one can still carry on performing one's duties (though only by effort and necessity) until one simply collapses . . . Recently the chief doctor (a dentist) simply declared me "serviceable" and threatened to give all the guards their commissions and declare them fit for field service! One just has to swallow this prolonged injustice together with all the rigours of one's duties. And I must give you a few details of these duties so that you can understand just why I am so urgently trying to alter my position: Report for duty at 6.45 am and command an hour's physical training, then march off to an exercise field where I have to exercise with the rest until 10 or half past, then back to the barracks to feed: the meat is alright, but nothing else is, since it's all prepared with old mutton fat. Mutton, by the way, is served up once or twice a week, abominably cooked. At about 12 we march off to the guard-house, which happens to be half-an-hour away. Activity in the guard-house equals nought. Sitting around for twenty-four hours in a little room saturated with tobacco smoke, with ten or twelve recruits. Every two hours I have to take one of them out—that is, collect the guard who is on duty and put someone in his place. So this goes on from 12.30 pm to 12.30 pm on the following day. In the night I can sleep for four hours, but this is reduced to three because it does not get quiet until 10 pm. At 1 I have to get up off my plank and perform my senseless duties without interruption until mid-day. You can imagine how I feel, how I have to fight off sleep, drink huge quantities of black coffee so as not to drop off in a sitting position. . . .'

At the end of May 1916 Berg at last obtained his transfer to an office at the Ministry of War and there he remained until the end of the war (November 1918). He used to describe his work as 'imprisonment' or 'slavery', but nevertheless, he could some-times enjoy an extended leave—which he would spend in intensive work on *Wozzeck*. In the summer of 1917 he had already begun on the composition (Act II, scene 2), although the text was not yet finished. On 19th August 1918 he wrote to Webern about his progress with the work; the following two sentences are of general interest: 'I cannot say whether or not I am pleased with what I have written, but I do feel warmth in writing it, and it runs from my hand more easily than I would have thought after such a long break . . . What touches me so closely is not only the fate of this poor man persecuted and exploited by all the world, but also the unbelievably con-centrated mood of the individual scenes . . .' His remarks about the extensive use of *Sprechstimme* (speech-singing) in the opera are also important. For example, he intended such characters as the doctor or the captain to express themselves only melodramatically; a resolution that he abandoned in the final version of the work.

Schönberg's presence in Vienna (as a civilian since Novem-ber 1917) was also very important to Berg. Schönberg at this time was realizing his new ideas about musical pedagogy. Besides his 'Seminar for Composition' (which he kept up until 1920) he carried out a very meaningful experiment in the spring of 1918: he directed ten public rehearsals—*not* followed by a concert performance—of his Chamber Symphony, Opus 9. Berg's contribution to this experiment was a thematic analysis of the work, which Universal Edition published in May 1918. A new epoch in Berg's career began with his appointment as director of performances to the 'Verein für musikalische Privataufführungen' (Society for musical private performances), a society founded in Vienna in November 1918 under Schön-berg's presidency.

Second Interlude

The purpose of this society, founded in November 1918, is to provide Arnold Schönberg with the possibility of personally carrying out his intention of giving artists and art-lovers a real and accurate knowledge of modern music.

One circumstance which contributes to a large extent to the relationship of the public to modern music, is that any impres-sion that they receive of it is inevitably one of un-clarity. The public is unclear about the purpose, the direction, the intention, the world of expression, the method of expression, the value, the nature and the aim of the works. The performances are for the most part unclear. And in particular the public's con-sciousness of its needs and desires is unclear. The consequence is that the works are valued, respected, praised and welcomed, or disregarded, censured and rejected, all on account of one single effect, which proceeds equally from all of them: *on account of un-clarity.*

In the long run, this cannot satisfy anybody worthy of atten-tion—no serious author, and none of the better members of an audience. The desire to achieve clarity at last, and thus take into account such needs and desires as are justified, this was one of the reasons that moved Arnold Schönberg to found the society.

Three things are necessary for the achievement of this aim:

1. Clear, well-prepared performances.
2. Frequent repetitions.
3. The performances must be withdrawn from the corrupting influence of publicity; that is, they must not be inspired by a

spirit of competition, and must be independent of applause and expressions of disapproval.

This points up the important difference that is apparent when we compare the task of this society with that of normal present-day concert life, which the society intends to keep definitely at a distance. For in the case of the latter

1. the work has to make do, for better or worse, with a fixed number of rehearsals—always too few—and it is signifi-cant that they generally do 'make do', though more often 'for worse' than 'for better'. Whereas the works performed by the society shall receive as many rehearsals as are necessary to achieve the greatest possible clarity and fulfil all the author's intentions respecting the work. Even if this necessitates a num-ber of rehearsals that has no equal in the musical profession today (such as is the case—to pick out one example—in study-ing one of Mahler's symphonies; twelve rehearsals, most of them of four hours, were necessary for the first performance, and a further two were needed before the repetition), if the fundamental requirements for a good reproduction are not satisfied, a work cannot and must not be performed in the society.

To make such extensive study possible, the performers will be chosen for the most part from amongst the young and less known, who place themselves at the society's disposal out of interest in the work. Performers whom fame has made expen-sive will be used only in cases where the work specifically requires them. A principle of selection as strict as this will exclude that species of virtuosity that sees the work to be per-formed not as an end in itself but merely as a means to an end—an end that can never be in harmony with the aims of the society, namely: a display of virtuosity and individuality that is far from the matter in hand, and the attainment of a purely personal success. Such things are made impossible by the ex-clusion, mentioned above, of any expression of appreciation, disapproval or gratitude. The only success that an artist can achieve here is the one that ought to be the most important;

success in having made the work, and thus the author, com/prehensible to his hearers.

A thoroughly prepared performance of this kind provides a reasonable guarantee that the work will be rightly understood. By the introduction of weekly meetings (at that time, every Sunday morning from 10 to 12 in the small Musikvereinssaal) a still more effective means to this end is provided, namely

2. the frequent repetition of every work. Moreover, to ensure regular attendance at the meetings, the programmes will not be announced in advance.

Only when these two requirements are met—thorough study and frequent repetition—can clarity take the place of un/clarity (which is usually the sole impression to be retained after a single performance); only then can a relationship to the work corres/ponding to the intentions of the work be established—a process of familiarization with the style and language, and finally a degree of familiarity that is generally only attainable after study/ing the work oneself. Such a degree of familiarity could be claimed for the present/day concert public only in the case of the most frequently played classical works.

The third point necessary for the achievement of the society's aims is fulfilled by the fact that the performances are not public; guests, with the exception of those from abroad, are not ad/mitted, and members of the society are obliged to refrain from any public pronouncement on the subject of the performances and activities of the society. In particular, members are asked neither to write nor provide inspiration for reviews, notices or discussions in periodic printed papers.

This non/publicity of the meetings is required by the quasi/pedagogic aspirations of the society, and coincides with its intention of providing the performed works merely with good performances—i.e. they must be content with whatever effect proceeds from the music itself. It is not the aim of the society to make propaganda for the works and their authors.

For this reason no particular direction will be preferred, and only the worthless will be excluded. What is to be presented is all modern music from Mahler and Strauss to the most recent, who do not get a sufficient chance to state their case.

Generally speaking it is the society's aim to present its mem/ bers with such works as are suited to show the most characteris/ tic and, as far as possible, accessible aspect of a composer's work. Besides songs, piano pieces, chamber music and works for small chorus, it has therefore been decided to take orchestral works into consideration. The society does not as yet possess the means to perform these in their original form, so to start with they can only be offered in the form of good, well/rehearsed arrangements for piano (four to eight hands). But: faced with such a task, it was possible to make a virtue of necessity. Namely: it is possible in this way to hear and judge modern orchestral works, stripped of the sound effects produced only by an orchestra, i.e. stripped of all sensual resources. This disarms the common objection, that this music is effective only on account of its more or less rich and ingenious instrumentation, and lacks those properties hitherto characteristic for good music: melodies, harmonic richness, polyphony, perfection of form, architecture, etc.

Taken from the society's prospectus, written by Berg in February 1919

FROM THE END OF THE WAR TO THE
PREMIÈRE OF 'WOZZECK'

The 'new epoch' in Berg's artistic activity that began at the end
of 1918 is characterized by stronger leanings towards the musical profession and work as a teacher. In a letter of 28th December 1919 to his mother at the Berghof he speaks of his work as
performance director of the Society (piano arrangements, direction of rehearsals, organizational work) for which he received
a monthly salary of 400 Kronen, and of three pupils who provide him with 450 Kronen monthly. A contribution from his
family circle raises his total income to 1,250 Kronen monthly—
a handsome sum in itself, but its purchasing power decreased
continually as a result of growing inflation. For the rest, his
time—he still often had to put up with physical suffering and
was not completely recovered from the rigours of the war—
was claimed by two activities: the management of seven Viennese houses owned by the family, and the carrying out of commissions for Universal Edition (the most recent was a
thematic analysis of Schönberg's symphonic poem 'Pelleas and
Melisande' which appeared in May 1920).

The reason we have seen fit to give this outline of Berg's
financial situation at that time is as follows: a conflict between
him and his family had been smouldering for some time, the
chief bone of contention being the management of the family's
Berghof property. All other measures having failed, his mother
asked Berg in a very drastic manner to take over the management. After a lot of argument—for he saw his whole existence
as a musician endangered—he gave in and in January 1920
moved into the Berghof. There he fulfilled his managing duties
with the exactitude and regularity that had become a second

nature to him; numerous documents provide evidence of this. But other texts show his desperation at having to engage in an activity so foreign to his nature. In a letter of 25th January 1920 to Webern, speaking of a performance of the latter's orchestral pieces in the Society (Berg's Four Pieces for Clarinet and Piano, Opus 5 had been heard in the Society for the first time—the composer being present—on 17th October 1919): 'I think of them a lot and frequently. I know them all too slightly, but in my memory they stand great and untouchably holy, like very few things in music, or in art in general. When will I hear them? Here I am *so far away* from these things, so abandoned by all good souls that often—forgive me this sin— I am *quite blind* to the magnificence of these winter days. I can-not explain why it is so, for the sight of a tree on the Ringstrasse is capable of rousing me to transports of enthusiasm for nature, but there it is. My senses, nerves and spiritual forces are all so blunted that I cannot even read a good book—don't even want to . . . A hundred times a day I ask myself what I am doing here . . . It is as though I had been "detailed" to come here by some power just as questionable as the militia in the war.'

However, two months later Berg could already send news of the approaching end of his exile in Kärnten. The Berghof had been sold. In May 1920 Berg was back in Vienna, and left it in future only for stays in the country (Steiermark or Kärnten) and short journeys to performances of his works or representa-tive conferences.

But before he left Kärnten he wrote Webern a six-page letter on 16th March containing a detailed outline of his plans for the future. In particular he speaks of the impossibility of com-bining his work as performance director of the Society with his other activities, which ensure him a living. He says at one point: 'I would like to devote myself completely to "writing about music", and also making piano reductions, etc. Schön-berg's works are crying out for all that, and I think I can do something in this line that is on a higher level than my work in the Society, for which I lack so much. . . . A type of work

that I would like to make into a regular job, not just the
occasional pot-boiler. In this way it would also be possible—
so I believe—to have a regular income. And I quite forgot:
besides this I must give as many lessons as possible! Composing?? Yes, that would be very nice. Perhaps one or two
months in the summer!!'

Berg set out on his intended career as a 'writer about music'
with a big polemical article against certain musico-aesthetic
remarks of Hans Pfitzner's; the article appeared in June 1920
in 'Musikblättern des Anbruch' published by Universal
Edition, and attracted considerable attention. We reprint it
here in full on *page 205*. On the basis of this success, Emil
Hertzka, director of Universal Edition, wanted to make
Berg editor of the magazine. Berg accepted the offer for 1st September 1920, but soon he began to have serious reservations
about the business, and on 14th August wrote to Webern from
Trahütten (where he had retired for the summer and was
making his 'first attempts at composition'—on *Wozzeck*):
'Believe me, I too regard the near future with fear and trembling. Will I be able to defy all resistance—Hertzka, the publisher's interests, Dr Schneider [editor of 'Anbruch' in Berlin]
—avoiding clashes, making no enemies? That's how Hertzka
imagines it! Will I be in a position to make absolutely no concessions? That's the negative side! And what about the positive
side: Will I really be able to do what is needful . . . just to get
the articles together to fill such a book, and a fortnight later
another one, and so on twenty times a year! My activity so far
has had practically no result. Believe me: I've spent so many
sleepless nights wishing I had never laid a finger on "Anbruch"
. . . Yes! when it comes to writing what suits me and publishing
it wherever I can get it accepted!— But, to take over the whole
management in such a slippery—almost journalistic—field.
Truly, if I didn't *have* to do it, if I didn't stand before the
necessity of scraping some means of existence, I would write
to Hertzka today and throw the whole thing over, come what
might, and spend the winter here and compose my opera and

finish the instrumentation. But as it is, I have to stake my immediate future (or my whole future?) on a "career" (horrible word) that means nothing to me but the bare possibility of existence; so from 1st September I throw myself into the arms of the public.'

After these sentences he writes: 'Seeing the matter from this point of view you will understand my actions of the last few days: I have obtained some money from the sale of a couple of antiques from the house, and used this money for the publica/ tion of my quartet and the clarinet pieces. Besides these two, I have had the sonata and songs (Opus 2) reprinted with numerous corrections. I consider it *necessary*—having decided, having had to decide to venture into the public eye—that com/ positions of mine should be available, since after all I am a composer. Had I not made that decision I would gladly dispense with such matters and be satisfied with the joys and pains of composing. So please don't think, for heaven's sake, that I have acted out of ambition in publishing my works myself instead of waiting patiently for something to appear of its own accord.'

Shortly afterwards, the piano reduction of the last of the Altenberg songs (Opus 4, No. 5) did appear 'of its own accord' (i.e. without Berg's collaboration) in the second special number of 'Junge Tonkunst' of the Dresden *avant garde* maga/ zine 'Menschen' edited by Paul Hasenclever (4th year, 1921, No. 5/6).

Berg was still working for 'Anbruch' in 1921. But none of his own contributions appeared in the magazine after the rejec/ tion of his article (completed end of August 1920) 'Two papers—A contribution to the brief on Schönberg and the critics'. The article was rejected probably out of consideration for the sensibilities of the Viennese critics who were castigated therein. Later Berg gave me the manuscript of the article for my small musical magazine '23', but it proved too long. It appears here for the first time unabridged on *page 219*.

After his two articles for 'Anbruch' Berg's career as 'writer about music' (at least in the form envisaged by him in the

quoted letter to Webern) was over. His later writings are con⁄
cerned only with homage to Schönberg, commentaries on his
own works, and personal appreciations of artists who were
close to him. Even the radio dialogue 'What is Atonal?',
published by me for the first time in 1930 and frequently re⁄
printed, is chiefly apologetic in character.

Against his decision as stated to Webern, Berg worked
intensively for the Society in the first half of 1921. We have
evidence of this in two long letters written to his fellow pupil
Erwin Stein, in which he speaks very critically of certain hap⁄
penings within the management of the Society. The crisis seems
to have reached its climax at the end of May with two public
concerts—one was a reading of Schönberg's 'Jakobsleiter'
poem by the actor Wilhelm Klitsch, the other was an 'Evening
of Waltzes'—and two internal meetings. Berg writes to Stein
on the subject on 2nd June: 'The amount of work contributed
by all concerned was enormous. During this time I was work⁄
ing fourteen hours a day and more for the Society. Then the
indescribable heat! I am amazed that my health sustained it,
what with the frightful number of difficulties.'

The 'Waltz evening' is a story in itself: For the purpose of
improving the ruined finances of the Society, Schönberg had
instrumentated two waltzes by Johann Strauss—the Lagoon
Waltz and 'Rosen aus dem Süden'—for string quartet, piano
and harmonium, and had further commissioned Berg and
Webern to do likewise. Berg arranged the waltz 'Wine,
Women and Song' and Webern arranged the 'Schatzwalzer'
from the *Gypsy Baron*. After the performance, in which Berg
played the harmonium, the manuscripts were auctioned. Berg
wrote Stein a detailed description of the concert, which resulted
in a considerable gain. Berg's waltz was given back to him by
the purchaser.

On 21st July 1921 Berg tells Stein of the foundation of the
Kolisch Quartet which was to play so important a part in
spreading the work of the second Viennese school. The letter
closes with the following important sentences: 'And I believe

that what is *accomplished* is more important than the *human being* [who accomplishes]. Perhaps the human being is merely to be "cultivated" with a view to obtaining the highest possible accomplishments from him. This at least has always been the only reason I did anything for my health. In this I was thinking of course of the highest accomplishment in composi' tion and not of matters connected with the Society. I've often thought that taking a walk or some other leisurely pastime would be more desirable for me than *those* matters. But there is probably a reason for that too.'

The fate of the Society—in the summer of 1921 Berg was still taking a lively interest in it from afar (Trahütten)—was decided in the autumn of that year; the rapid depreciation of Austrian currency forced its dissolution. Now Berg turned his whole energy to the opera, which was to occupy all his thoughts for some time to come.

On 21st September 1921 he writes to Webern that the com' position of the last scene of *Wozzeck* has begun. The short score of the work was finished in October 1921 and he was ready to begin work on the instrumentation and the vocal score. Before he did so, however, Berg travelled to Frankfurt and Darmstadt and played the work from the short score to the opera directors in those cities—with no result. The instrumenta' tion was finished in April 1922. The vocal score—made by Berg's pupil Fritz Heinrich Klein—went to press at the end of July 1922. At the instigation of Alma Maria Mahler—with whom the Bergs had enjoyed friendly relations for some time past—Berg was bold enough to publish the vocal score inde' pendently. In January 1923 he announced the publication: 'The score is 230 pages long, large quarto size, costs 150,000 Austrian Kronen (20 Swiss Francs) and can be obtained direct from me.' He sent the advertisement to his fellow pupil Erwin Stein on 8th January and enclosed a calendar page with the pro' verb 'Art looks for Bread'. In the accompanying letter he wrote: 'Do you know of anyone who would buy the score? Perhaps on your recommendation. The production was enormously

expensive and I'll never be able to persuade a publisher to pay
for it, so I would like to sell a number of them beforehand
for my own account. That's the reason for today's calendar
page motto.' This occasioned the remark of another fellow
pupil: 'No publisher even thought of publishing the monster;
the vocal score was in hot demand only amongst his good
friends, and they got it free.'

Erwin Stein was the first to write about the opera, in 'Anbruch' at the end of January 1923. Meanwhile Berg had sent
off copies of the vocal score to all the most important German-
language opera companies and musical magazines. The result
of this action was not what the composer wished—i.e. accep-
tance of the work for performance by one of the opera companies—but violent polemics in the Berlin monthly magazine
'Die Musik'. The magazine first printed (April 1923) a
thorough evaluation by Ernst Viebig ('Alban Berg's *Wozzeck*'
together with a musical supplement 'Wiegenlied der Marie').
This was followed up by a furious attack by Emil Petschnig
('Atonal opera-composition'), which Berg countered in the
same number with a brief, matter-of-fact rectification ('The
musical forms in my opera *Wozzeck*'). We reproduce here the
opening and closing words of the last-mentioned: 'It is far
from my intention to counter Mr Emil Petschnig's views,
musico-theoretical and otherwise—every bar of my music does
this much better than any words. I just wish to correct some of
the crassest of the untruths in which his article abounds. . . .
One may believe me when I say that this and other musical
forms have been successfully executed in the places where they
were intended, and also that I am able to demonstrate their
rightness and legitimacy more thoroughly and therefore more
persuasively than has been possible here. Anyone who wishes
to be convinced of this should apply to me; I am ready and
willing.'

A few events outside the sphere of *Wozzeck* occurred in the
middle of 1923. Präludium and Reigen from the Three
Orchestral Pieces, Opus 6 were premièred on 5th June in

Berlin as part of an 'Austrian Music Week'. The conductor was Webern and the reception friendly; the critics spoke of the influence of Debussy. On 18th July Berg wrote to Webern about his 'industrious but difficult' work on a concerto for piano and violin accompanied by ten (!) wind instruments. This was to turn into the chamber concerto and he eventually had to use thirteen wind instruments (see the dedicatory letter to Schönberg on *page* 143). On 2nd August Berg achieved a great and generally recognized success in Salzburg during the first chamber music festival organized by the International Society for Contemporary Music (founded the previous year) with his String Quartet, Opus 3, played by the Havemann Quartet.

In Salzburg he also met Hermann Scherchen, who encouraged him to take some pieces out of *Wozzeck* and make a cycle for concert performance, and then send it in to the 'Allgemeinen Deutschen Musikverein'. The resulting triptych achieved a strong spiritual unity, as Berg chose chiefly the music written for the main female character, Marie. The three fragments were performed in this form on 15th June 1924 at the 54th Music Festival of the 'Allgemeinen Deutschen Musikverein' which took place in Frankfurt. The conductor was Hermann Scherchen, and the soloist Beatrice Sutter-Kottlar. There were a number of difficulties in the rehearsal, but Berg was able to write to Webern on 17th June that 'everything was magnificent in the end: the performance itself and especially the singer. The success grew from rehearsal to rehearsal, and in the public performances (dress rehearsal and concert) it turned into a great victory: public, musicians and the press were all won over.' The *Wozzeck*-cycle really did become the sensation of the festival, and from that point on its composer was generally regarded by German musicians as an artistic phenomenon of great significance.

The première of the whole opera had already been fixed before this triumphant success: Erich Kleiber, general musical director of the Berlin State Opera since the autumn of 1923

(Berg did not know him at this stage) had been in Vienna in January 1924. Berg had had his pianist friend Eduard Steuer/ mann play the opera _Wozzeck_ to him in the office of the Konzerthaus. Kleiber told me later that after the second scene he had cried out: 'It's settled! I am going to do the opera in Berlin, even if it costs me my job!' Almost exactly two years later—on 14th December 1925—Kleiber directed the première of _Wozzeck_ in the Berlin State Opera.

Before we come to speak of this event—an event of the highest importance not only for Berg but for the whole history of opera—we have to consider another matter that occupied Berg intensely in the summer of 1924. Universal Edition plan/ ned a special number of 'Anbruch' devoted to Schönberg on the occasion of the master's fiftieth birthday, and Berg took over the editorship. He himself contributed the closing article: 'Why is Schönberg's music so Difficult to Understand?' Quite apart from the high musico/literary value of the article, Berg's analysis of the first ten bars of Schönberg's First String Quartet (Opus 7 in D minor) is so characteristic of the exactitude of his musical thinking and of his whole didactic method that we have seen fit to reproduce the article in full as documentary testimony to Berg's theoretical and teaching activity (_see p._ 189). Yet a few more significant events before the epoch/making première of _Wozzeck_: First, the completion of the Chamber Concerto on 9th February 1925. Second, the drafting of a very spirited apologia for Schönberg ('A committed answer to a non/committal questionnaire') in the 1926 yearbook of Universal Edition, and third, the commencement of work on the Lyric Suite for String Quartet. Berg wrote to Webern about the two last in a letter of 18th September 1925 from Trahütten: 'Yesterday I completed the little article for the UE yearbook and sent it off. It is an answer to the question "Out/ look on music in the next twenty/five years". The whole is more whimsical than scholarly, but my unshakable convic/ tion of the _only possible_ answer—namely "Schönberg"—comes through _in all seriousness._ And now if I can only accomplish

Staats-Theater
Opernhaus

Berlin, Montag, den 14. Dezember 1925

14. Karten-Reservesatz.
(Außer Abonnement.)

Uraufführung:

Georg Büchners

Wozzeck

Oper in drei Akten (15 Szenen) von **Alban Berg**.
Musikalische Leitung: General-Musikdirektor Erich Kleiber.
In Szene gesetzt von Franz Ludwig Hörth.

Wozzeck . . . . Leo Schützendorf
Tambourmajor . . . . Fritz Soot
Andres . . . . Gerhard Witting
Hauptmann . . . . Waldemar Henke
Doktor . . . . Martin Abendroth
1. Handwerksbursch . . . . Ernst Osterkamp
2. Handwerksbursch . . . . Alfred Borchardt
Der Narr . . . . Marcel Noë

Marie . . . . Sigrid Johanson
Margret . . . . Jessyka Koettrik
Mariens Knabe . . . . Ruth Iris Witting
Soldat . . . . Leonhard Kern
Soldaten und Burschen, Mägde und Dirnen, Kinder.

Gesamtausstattung: P. -Aravantinos.

Technische Einrichtung: Georg Linnebach.

Nach dem 2. Akt findet eine längere Pause statt.

Kein Vorspiel.

Den Besuchern der heutigen Vorstellung wird das neu erschienene Heft der „Blätter der Staatsoper" unentgeltlich verabfolgt.

successfully the most difficult of all leaps—that into the beginning of a composition!'

There was a great deal of unrest in the Berlin State Opera
during the weeks preceding the première of *Wozzeck*. After an
extended crisis, the manager—Max von Schillings—resigned in
November 1925, and after his departure Kleiber's position was
also precarious for some time. All this sharpened the opposition
to the opera in some quarters—already in advance it had been
cried down as 'ultra-modern'. The tension was heightened by
rumours of an unimaginable number of rehearsals—in reality
thirty-four orchestral rehearsals and fourteen ensemble rehearsals
—and of the immeasurable demands to be made on the singers
and theatre personnel. This tension was discharged in demonstrations—mild enough at the dress rehearsal, but violent at the
première itself—against the work and the performers.

Hans Heinsheimer—later director of a publishing house in
New York; at that time director of the opera department of
Universal Edition—has written a very dramatic account of his
experiences at the première of *Wozzeck* and the conclusions
that he later drew from them in a book of memoirs published
twelve years ago ('Menagerie in F-sharp major', Zürich 1953).
Among other things, he writes: 'At the première there were
fisticuffs and verbal duels between the stalls and the boxes,
derisive laughter, hissing and shrill whistling; for a time it
seemed as though the enemies of the work might overwhelm
the few—finally victorious—adherents of the composer. Did
we—we who applauded and shouted so valiantly until the
lights were turned out and the safety curtain was lowered—
did we really understand what was new, great and revolu-
tionary about the work? Perhaps a few did, but most of us did
not. So what was it that moved us so? There is an inner ear—
an invisible receiving apparatus—which may not necessarily
perceive all the technical refinements of a composition, but is
nevertheless stirred in some magical way by beauty, power and
strength, and can distinguish between the resounding steps of
the giant and the hasty gallop of the busy dwarf. The violent

differences of opinion continued in the newspapers for days and weeks. On the one side high praise and humble recogni-tion of the work's greatness and its creator's importance, and on the other, hate-filled and almost hysterical condemnation. We collected all the opinions together in a little book under the title "Alban Berg's *Wozzeck* and the Music Critics" and left it to the inescapable judgment of history to decide who was right and who was wrong.'

We quote here one review *contra* and one *pro* from the little book mentioned by Heinsheimer.

The following excerpt is from the review by Paul Zschorlich entitled 'Stuttering at the State Opera': 'Leaving the State Opera House *Unter den Linden* last evening, I had the feeling that I was not leaving a public institute of art but a public mad-house. On the stage, in the orchestra, in the stalls: a lot of madmen . . . *Wozzeck* by Alban Berg was the battle-cry—the work of a chinaman from Vienna. For these massed attacks and convulsions of instruments had nothing to do with Euro-pean music and its development . . . The applause from the stalls is nothing other than a cracking lie. But what attitude does the master criminal of this work strike? There are only two possibilities: either he recognizes laws, forms, skill and submission to higher inspiration in music, or he denies every-thing that has existed, that has developed and been created in hallowed hours, he scoffs at forms and laws, he despises all the great masters, he scribbles down whatever leaks out of his pen, he is completely unscrupulous, he builds confidently on the stupidity and mercifulness of his fellow men, and for the rest relies on God in Heaven and the Universal Edition. In the whole vocal score of *Wozzeck* I cannot find a single instance that would indicate honest and genuine inspiration . . . In Berg's music there is not the slightest trace of melody. There are only scraps and shreds, sobs and belches. Harmonically, the work cannot be discussed, for every single thing sounds wrong . . . The instrumentation is varied. He runs through all the possibilities between the last gasp of violin harmonics and the bass tuba's meanest grunt. A whole zoological garden is opened up . . . I consider Alban Berg a musical impostor, and a treacherously dangerous composer. Yes, one seriously has to consider the question, whether and to what extent activity in music can be criminal. This is a matter of a capital crime in the field of music . . .'

H. H. Stückenschmidt reports: 'It is difficult to do justice to the strange perfection and uniqueness of this work within the limits of a review. There can never before have been chosen for an opera a libretto whose literary value so completely corres' ponds to the possibilities of musical interpretation as does that of this magnificent fragment by George Büchner. . . . Berg has succeeded in writing a music for this libretto that not only does not diminish the value of the literary work but actually enhances it to an unheard'of degree. It is a music that brings latent matters to the surface and uncovers the most secret psychological factors without waiving the most important things, namely the dramatic conception and the musical unity. The fact that Berg has done this is evidence of genius, and places him right next to the most important music'dramatists of our time . . . Not only was the evening the greatest sensation of the season, it was a significant event in the history of music' drama in general. . . .'

What Berg himself thought about the problem of opera in general, and in particular about the solution presented by him in *Wozzeck*, may be learnt from the following interlude—a text that Berg wrote three years after the memorable *Wozzeck* première in Berlin.

Third Interlude

Pro mundo:
Asked a similar question on the occasion of a recent modern opera première, I wrote the following in a programme book. In it I believe I have also stated my position with regard to the 'problem of opera' in general.

'What do you think about the contemporary further development of opera?'—just the same as I think about every development in matters of art: namely, that one day a master-piece will be written that points so clearly into the future that one will be able to speak—on the basis of this work's exist-ence—of a "further development of opera". The use of "contem-porary" means—such as cinema, revue, loudspeakers, jazz—guarantees only that such a work is contemporary. But that cannot be called a real step forward; after all, this is the point we have reached, and we can't get further on simply by being here.

Before one can say of the art-form of opera that it has de-veloped further—as happened for example with Monteverdi, Lully, Gluck, Wagner and finally Schönberg's stage works—some means are necessary other than merely bringing in the latest skills and everything that happens to be popular.

But does there always have to be "further development"? Isn't it sufficient to have the opportunity of making beautiful music for good theatre works, or, to put it better, to make such good music that—in spite of that—good theatre is the result?

This brings me to my own personal position with regard to the 'problem of opera', which I need to speak about for the sake of putting right an error about my said position that cropped up as soon as my opera *Wozzeck* appeared and has since become widespread. So I may be forgiven this

Pro domo:

Never in my wildest dreams would I have wished to reform, with the composition of *Wozzeck*, the art-form of opera. Far as that was from my intentions when I began to compose the work, I was just as far from considering what then emerged as being a model for any further operatic composition—whether mine or another composer's—and I never assumed nor even expected that *Wozzeck* could 'start a school' in that sense.

Apart from my desire to make good music, to fulfil, musically, the spiritual content of Büchner's immortal drama, to transpose his poetic language into a musical one,—apart from these things I had nothing else in mind at the moment when I decided to write an opera, nothing else in mind even as regards the technique of composition, than to render to the theatre what is the theatre's, and that means to shape the music in such a way that it is aware in every moment of its duty to serve the drama. Still further: the music must produce everything that the play needs for its transposition into the reality of the boards; and this requires from the composer that he carry out all the most important tasks of an ideal director. And all this without prejudicing the usual absolute (purely musical) justification of such music; without prejudicing the music's own life, which may not be hindered by anything extramusical.

That this was done by calling in musical forms that are more or less old (which is regarded as one of my main supposed operatic reforms) was a decision that made itself.

The mere necessity of making a selection from Büchner's twenty-six loose scenes—some of them fragmentary—for my libretto, set me a task more musical than literary; I had to avoid repetitions in so far as they were not capable of variation musically, and further I had to pull these scenes together and string them along, and collect them in groups for the different

9 With Anton von Webern, *c.* 1923

10, 11   Sets by P. Aravantinos for the première of *Wozzeck* in Berlin on 14th December 1925. Act I, scene 2 (*above*) and Act III, scene 2 (*below*)

acts of the opera. This task could only be solved by recourse to the laws of musical architecture, and not to the laws of dramaturgy.

But the problems of shaping the fifteen scenes that were left over after the process of selection and condensation in the rich and varied manner which alone could guarantee the necessary musical definition and penetration—this problem was what really forbade the usual method of continuously 'composing through' the scenes, with reference merely to their literary content. No absolute music, however rich in structure and however aptly it illustrated the dramatic action, could have prevented a feeling of musical monotony from making itself felt after only a small number of scenes composed in this manner. A feeling of reluctance that would only be sharpened into boredom by a series of a dozen *entr'actes* that could offer nothing —formally—but the fulfilment of the consequences of such a musically illustrative method of writing. And boredom is the last thing one should be permitted to feel in the theatre!

Since I gave heed to the imperious demand that each of these scenes and each of the accompanying *entr'actes* (whether in the form of preludes, postludes, transitions or interludes) should not only have their own unmistakable profiles but should also be well-rounded and complete, it came about naturally that I called in everything that guaranteed such a degree of characterization on the one hand and completeness on the other. This is how the much-discussed requisition of old and new musical forms—including forms that are usually used only in absolute music—come about.

The introduction of these forms into the field of opera on such a large scale may have been unusual, perhaps new. But after what I have said here, it is clear that there was no particular merit in it! So I can—and must—decidedly refute the contention that I have reformed the art-form of opera with such innovations.

But I do not wish to belittle my work with this declaration —others who know the work less can do that much better than

I—so I will gladly divulge something which I do consider to be my own exclusive merit:

However much one may know about the musical forms to be found in this opera—how strictly and logically it is all 'worked out', how ingeniously planned in all its details . . . from the moment when the curtain rises until it descends for the last time, there must not be anyone in the audience who notices anything of these various fugues and inventions, suite movements and sonata movements, variations and passacaglias. Nobody must be filled with anything else except the idea of the opera—which goes far beyond the individual fate of Wozzeck. And that—so I believe—I have achieved!

From the 'Neue Musik-Zeitung', Year 49, volume 9, Stuttgart 1928

THE PEAK OF HIS LIFE

The opera *Wozzeck* proclaimed itself directly to every unprejudiced listener as a full artistic achievement, and this was confirmed by the unexampled triumphal progress of the work, which initiated Berg's path to world fame. Even an apparently severe setback, like the first production of the opera to follow the Berlin première, could not inhibit the constant spread of the work.

The first hearing of the *Wozzeck* music in the composer's home town took place in 1926. The three fragments were successfully performed in Vienna on 13th March in a workers' symphony concert under the direction of Heinrich Jalowetz. The concert was repeated on 13th October. Berg's urgent desire to take up work on the string quartet that he had begun the previous year persuaded him to retire to Trahütten at the end of May—earlier than was his wont. Despite the severe physical illnesses (stomach trouble and asthma) which necessitated an interruption of his sojourn in the country, and despite the urgent job of correcting the score of *Wozzeck* and making a piano score of the Chamber Concerto, Berg managed to complete the composition of the Lyric Suite for String Quartet early in October. On his return to Vienna he had only the fair copy still to make.

Shortly afterwards he went to Prague where *Wozzeck* was to be performed on 11th November in the Czech National Theatre under the direction of Otokar Ostrčil. The première and the first repeat performance enjoyed great artistic success, thanks to the freshness and naturalness of the actors. But at the second repeat performance there were demonstrations instigated by a few nationalistic newspapers. These were reported by the

'Frankfurter Zeitung' as follows: 'The performance was broken off after the second act; the theatre had to be cleared by police, and the fierce discussions continued outside the building. This resistance had been organized: the news that the Mayor of Prague and six box-subscribers had protested against the opera sufficed to call forth the sirens and whistles of a few young toughs during the delicate interludes of the work, and the curtain had to be rung down.' The higher authorities forbade further performances of the work 'in order to prevent further scandals'. All the artistic organizations of the city agreed on a general resolution and protested sharply against this measure, but to no avail. In Berlin the opera remained in the repertoire for two seasons, and was later revived twice—1929 and 1923— by Kleiber with new productions.

Berg wrote to Watznauer—who had been present at the Prague première—about the further occurrences in that city in a letter of 22nd November: 'The second performance was just as good as the first: a great success for the work, and the theatre was sold out. This gave the Czech nationalists and clerics no peace, and in the third performance they staged the scandal that you have certainly heard about. . . . The reviews were excellent, with the exception of that one political party—they wished to brand me "Alban (Aaron) Berg, the Jew from Berlin".' Shortly afterwards Berg had to tell this friend of his youth of the death of his mother; she had died in her sleep on 19th December, after following the events connected with *Wozzeck* in Berlin and Prague with lively interest.

The spectacular performance of *Wozzeck* in the Academic Theatre in Leningrad on 12th May overshadows the other important premières of Berg's recent works that took place early in 1927. The Lyric Suite was played in Vienna on 8th January by the Kolisch Quartet (who at that time were playing under the name 'The New Viennese String Quartet'), and the Chamber Concerto was conducted by Hermann Scherchen in Berlin on 20th March with Steffi Geyer (violin) and Walter Grey (piano) as soloists.

Berg himself tells of his impressions of Leningrad in two long-forgotten interviews: 'On the way from the station to my lodging house I was truly dismayed: my name and the name of my work stared down at me in giant letters from every street corner, every hoarding and every advertising pillar. That taught me straight away that in Leningrad a première is not a matter that concerns only a couple of experts whose reports then decree whether or not a larger public will interest itself in the following performances. Such an extensive involvement of the whole of a large city is rather alarming for one who is not used to it . . . I had come to Leningrad in rather an anxious frame of mind, and asked myself over and over again how the conductor and singers—none too familiar with the latest operatic music—would find their way around in my complicated score. I was in for a most pleasant surprise. Draschnikow, the conductor, had done excellent work. They had been studying the work for six months. There was a complete understudy cast—all equal in merit to the first cast. *Wozzeck* was sung with real *belcanto*. Yes, a modern opera needs just as nice singing as *Troubadour*! And the phrasing must be just as flexible. If these points are not observed the result is the same sort of silly impression as would be created if someone were to read aloud while completely ignoring the punctuation. I hardly need to emphasize that it was a stylized production; such things are a matter of course in Russia. The sets were designed by Radlow in extremely modern style. When I was working on the opera I never thought of a constructivist production, indeed I could not have done, for constructivism only asserted itself afterwards. But it was well suited to the work. The poet Kusmin's translation of the text was proclaimed masterly. I can report with satisfaction that the thing was a success and that the reviews were good without exception. A toast proposed by a young Russian composer at the banquet given in my honour is enough to show how they appreciate modern music in Russia: the toast ended "Bottoms up to Arnold Schönberg, the teacher of all living composers!" '

Severe physical illnesses (digestive organs, asthma) cast a shadow over the rest of 1927. Berg was not really in a condition to enjoy the triumphal journey of the Lyric Suite, which the Kolisch Quartet took on tour after the Baden-Baden chamber music festival in July 1927, nor the success of the Chamber Concerto at the ISCM festival in Frankfurt on 4th July. And his creative musical work came to a halt. The only thing that occupied him ceaselessly was the search for a new opera text; he had started looking for one immediately after finishing *Wozzeck*.

He was constantly examining a great many subjects, but in the end two possibilities came to the fore: Gerhart Hauptmann's glassworks fairy-tale 'Und Pippa tanzt', a text that had strongly attracted him as much as twenty years previously, and Frank Wedekind's 'Lulu Tragedy', which reminded him of the activities of Karl Kraus (*see p. 156*). As early as 1926 he had corresponded with Hauptmann's publishers about a possible setting of 'Pippa'. They had told him that the poet was pre-pared to give him compositional rights in the work, but not exclusive rights. This did not satisfy Berg, and although he had already made a complete arrangement of the text for his pur-poses, he decided to abandon all thoughts of composing 'Und Pippa Tanzt'. At the end of January 1928 he made the per-sonal acquaintance of the poet in Rapallo. Hauptmann ex-pressed his regret that Berg had not approached him directly. But by this time the decision—influenced to some extent by the advice of close friends—had already fallen on 'Lulu', and in the spring of 1928 Berg began the arrangement of the text. This work consisted chiefly in shortening the text, but he was to make many further changes in the course of composition.

Meanwhile, wishing to be represented in the concert halls by some work as yet unknown, Berg made an orchestral version of seven songs composed in the period from 1905 to 1908, originally for voice and piano. The new version was premièred in Vienna on 6th November 1928 in a concert organized by the 'Gesellschaft der Musikfreunde'. The conductor was Robert Heger, the soloist Claire Born.

My own first personal meeting with Berg took place three days before this première. I had for a long time been a great admirer of his. Now I had my first 'lesson' with him, and I would like to take this opportunity of making a more or less comprehensive report on his work as a teacher.

Schönberg said on one occasion: 'If you are in a position to observe the way Mahler ties his tie, you can learn more counter-point from this than you can in three years at the conservatory.' The profound seriousness behind these joking words was to strike me often when—after my initial period of study—I began to come to Berg more and more frequently outside my lessons, and was permitted to be at his side as a sort of 'famulus' in several more or less complicated situations of everyday life. The majority of the numerous letters he wrote to me deal with such matters, and they strengthen my devoted memory of this won-derful man and artist, who was truly 'great' even in the most apparently trivial things. Great in the way he looked at them and made them a part of his life. Controlled by a highly developed ironic awareness of himself coupled with benevolent good humour towards others, his noble way of living sustained him throughout the whole range of his activities, from tying his tie to considerations of the most difficult ethical and philo-sophical problems. I learnt more from the way he lived—even about his general attitude to music—than I could ever have learnt from instruction, even such instruction as he gave, which was often sprinkled with reminiscences of his own period of study with Schönberg.

The first time I was received as a student in his comfortable home in Hietzing, he offered me a cigarette at the beginning of our conversation. When I refused, saying that I was a non-smoker, he was profoundly disquieted and asked: 'But . . . how do you compose then?' He himself, in periods of intense work, smoked one cigarette after another (using—to his wife's disgust—the inside of the piano as an ashtray, and encouraging all pupils who smoked to do likewise) and he was visibly relieved when I revealed that I had given up composition on discovering that all my creative efforts had been mere imitations of the great composers of the past, and that what I wanted was to repeat the whole course of study that he had been through with Schönberg purely out of special interest in the method. He regarded this resignation of mine as a powerful proof—as he told me later, partly ironically, partly seriously—of my gifts as a music critic. However that may be, my confession brought me the following advantage: Berg was much freer and more open with me than he was with any of his other pupils, whom he did not wish to discourage by referring too frequently to his own works—he did not wish to harp on his superiority.

A lesson with Berg would generally run as follows: he would take the pupil's exercises and tentative compositions in the most friendly manner and lay them on the piano. Then he would let his eye run over them from the top, emitting plenty of exclamations of agreement and encouragement of a general sort, such as 'not bad', 'a good idea', 'not bad at all', 'good, good'. Then he would invite the pupil—who was naturally highly pleased with this praise—to sit next to him at the piano, and go through his work bar for bar and note for note, with the following result: after his corrections had been carried out—the pages usually looked like desolated battle-fields—a completely different composition emerged, with little in common with what the pupil had brought along. But he would never write a single note in the manuscript unless the pupil was genuinely convinced, and sanctioned it completely —not submitting merely to the authority of the brilliant teacher. The sharpest criticism he was ever heard to utter was 'You haven't quite heard that out yet!'

Berg treated his pupils similarly even when they were away from him. As evidence of this we have a letter written on 28th August 1929—just after the completion of the concert aria 'Der Wein'—addressed to Hans Erich Apostel, who had been commissioned by a Viennese concert pianist to write a piano sonata. Apostel had sent in the first sketch for the composition. 'Thank you, dear Apostel for your letter. Unfortunately I don't have time to give you the comprehensive answer that the letter requires. I say "unfortunately", because a *comprehensive* discussion of your sonata sketch would not create such an impression of rejection as when I simply say—that I don't find it very satisfactory. Nevertheless, to put it briefly: above all I miss a main theme, a real melodic idea. What you have put down in black and white is a mood—a very distinct one—but all the rest is sequences of one or two quite short motifs. The theme *must* begin *at least* at the double bar. Think of one—in the same mood—and then work on ahead with it as I always advise you: *develop*, do not write sequences, and *intensify*, and when it's exhausted, bring in something new. It will form a unity of its own accord, or one can help it along—either way it's a much easier matter than nursing a nothing, however rich in cross-references. And—do not occupy your mind with writing a piece "to order". Write the sonata in the way it occurs to you. You don't need to make any concessions; least of all for N. who is quite modern enough to "go along with you". And I'm sure she did not ask you for anything popular, —rather for something Apostular. When you realize this your dilemma will disappear and only the joy of working will be left. Start out without any inhibitions, bring to it whatever you are capable of in the way of craft,—and ideas about where and when you will be popular and where and when you will be schoolmasterly will never even occur to you. With my Aria it was just the same, in spite of the inescapable necessity of taking this particular voice and musicality into account. But that was what made it stimulating for me . . .'

However penetrating and conscientious was Berg's criticism of his pupil's products, it seemed mild and lenient compared with the criticism he brought to bear on his own works. Only thus is the relatively small number of his works and the much-discussed slowness with which he worked to be explained, and not by any meagreness or hesitancy in his musical ideas. These flowed in such fullness and intensity, as I myself often had occasion to observe, that he was hardly able to defend himself against them; he spent much more time viewing and considering these than he spent actually writing down his compositions. His highest law of creation was untiring 'hearing it out' over and over again, and he submitted even his completed works to this treatment over and over again, not just the works that he was in process of writing.

As an example of his constant re-proofing of completed works we may mention the two settings (1907 and 1925) of the poem 'Schliesse mir die Augen beide mit den lieben Händen zu' ('Close my two eyes with your dear hands') by Theodor Storm. Berg dedicated these two compositions—one of which is completely tonal, the other composed by means of the twelve-note technique—to Emil Hertzka, general director of Universal Edition, on the occasion of the twenty-fifth Jubilee of the publishing house. Since May 1927 Berg had been closely in-volved with Universal Edition through a contract for all his present and future works. He wrote that the dedication of the two songs was also intended to express the thought that the twenty-five years' activity of Universal Edition was just as important as 'the enormous distance that music has travelled from tonal composition to that 'with twelve notes related only to one another' (Schönberg's twelve-note technique), from the C major triad to the mother chord (the twelve-note chord dis-covered by Berg's pupil Fritz Heinrich Klein containing all eleven intervals), and it is to the lasting credit of Emil Hertzka that he was the only publisher to travel this distance right from the beginning'. In 1929 Berg gave me a facsimile of the dedica-tion copy of the two songs and gave me permission to publish them together with my first biographical article about him, which appeared in the Berlin magazine 'Die Musik' in February 1930. To this end the songs were engraved in Berlin from my copy. When Berg receive the brush-proofs he made such a large number of corrections—in six colours—that the compositions were significantly changed and the engraved plates were unusable. If the songs were to be published at all they would have to be engraved all over again. I happened to

be in Berlin when Bernhard Schuster—the editor of the magazine and a great admirer of Berg's work—received the corrected
proofs from Vienna. He had me called in and explained that
remaking the plates would mean a considerable material loss—
which he was quite ready to incur, however, because the brush-
proofs sprinkled all over with Berg's corrections was something
quite unique and gave him real pleasure. The new engraving
was carried out with such care that in the final printing Berg
found nothing whatever to complain of.

Such strict self-criticism explains Berg's clear consciousness
—free from any vain self-glorification—of the significance and
value of his works (the ones which he himself declared valid).
In this connection, I will never forget the following incident:
One of his works, I think it was the three *Wozzeck* fragments,
had enjoyed a great success with the public at a performance in
a large German industrial town. The reviews were also very
favourable; but one reviewer had tempered his praise with the
observation that Berg sometimes leaned rather too heavily on
the work of Mr X (X was the long-standing director of the
conservatory in that town, and a highly respected, strictly con-
servative composer). Berg was profoundly concerned at this
remark, and had all the published compositions of X sent to
him from the publishers—he had never heard a single note of
the man's music—and proceeded to study it thoroughly. On
one of my visits about this time I found the collected works of
Mr X all piled up in the room. Berg pointed to the stack and
said (he spoke his usual elegant, rather negligent Viennese):
'If I lean on that bloke, he'll fall over!'

But within his strong self-confidence he knew very well
where to draw the line. The following tragi-comic incident—
we are jumping ahead slightly in time—concerns the figure of
poor Wozzeck, the officer's servant who is humiliated and
hunted by his fellow men, the 'hero' of Berg's first opera. In the
summer of 1930, shortly after the première of *Wozzeck* at the
Vienna State Opera, the Austrian '*Tabak-regie*' (state tobacco
monopoly) had placed an announcement in the newspapers to

the effect that they would be bringing out a new product—a most expensive luxury cigarette—under the name 'Heliane', in memory of the opera by Erich Wolfgang Korngold produced at the Vienna State Opera, *Das Wunder der Heliane*. The previous year they had put a cigarette called 'Jonny' on the market, the name being derived from Křenek's opera *Jonny spielt auf*. Berg sent me the advertisement from his summer laboratorium in Kärnten and wrote: 'This announcement awakens an old wish of mine; I wish that a cheap—the cheapest —people's cigarette should carry the name Wozzeck (instead of some "honourable" title!) I can't be the one to set such an idea in motion. But how would it be if you, my dear Mr Reich, were to send one of your witty letters to the tobacco directors and suggest the idea. It recommends itself on account of the Jonny cigarettes (for an international clientèle) and the Heliane cigarettes (for the *haute volée*). Perhaps it would be advisable to mention the "popularity" of my opera, since the tobacco directors will probably confuse "Wozzeck" with the military conductor Wacek . . .' I wrote immediately to the Tabak-regie people, not only 'wittily' but 'musico-historically' as well. But my letter went unanswered and the composer's modest pipe-dream fizzled out.

In the first months of 1929 there were two performances that were important for the spreading of Berg's work throughout the world. In Berlin on 31st January Jascha Horenstein conducted the première of three movements (Nos. 2–4) from the Lyric Suite in an arrangement for string orchestra made by Berg. Soon these pieces were amongst the most widely known of Berg's works. Kleiber introduced Berg's music in the U.S.A. for the first time—the first time in the whole of the Americas— with these pieces and the *Wozzeck* fragments (1930 and 1931). In doing so he prepared the way for the American première of *Wozzeck*. The three pieces from the Lyric Suite were also the only work of Berg's to be played by the élite orchestra of his home town—the Vienna Philharmonic—during the com-poser's lifetime.

On 5th March 1929 there was a performance of *Wozzeck* in the little German provincial town of Oldenburg which was completely satisfactory, artistically and in every way. It was repeated numerous times. This finally put an end to the stories that were always being told about the 'insuperable difficulties of rehearsing' the opera. These difficulties were supposed to paralyse all other theatrical activities for a long period preceding the performance, so that the work could only be staged by the largest companies. The conductor Johannes Schüler proved, with exact statistics, that his performance could be produced with twelve general rehearsals and without interfering with normal theatrical work. On a postcard sent to his pupil Julius Schloss on the day after the première, Berg characterized the Oldenburg performance as 'A miracle! A veritable miracle!'

Schüler, the conductor, had shown such profound under/ standing in his production of *Wozzeck* that Berg decided to entrust the first performance of the Three Orchestral Pieces, Opus 6 to his hands. He had slightly touched up the instrumen/ tation in 1929. The concert took place in Oldenburg on 14th April 1930; the third piece (March) was heard for the first time ever. Ties of great friendship bound Berg to Johannes Schüler after the memorable première of *Wozzeck*. Schüler demonstrated his fidelity to the master with model performances of his works, and continued to do so after Berg's death.

The successful première in Oldenburg broke the spell that had lain on *Wozzeck* ever since the demonstrations in Berlin and Prague. In the period from the end of 1929 until Berg's death the opera was performed in the following cities: Essen, Aachen, Vienna, Düsseldorf, Königsberg, Lübeck, Liège, Amster/ dam, Cologne, Gera, Brunswick, Rotterdam, Darmstadt, Phila/ delphia, Frankfurt, Freiburg im Breisgau, Wuppertal, Leipzig, Zürich, New York, Chemnitz, Brussels, Mannheim, Brünn and London. In Oldenburg Berg had given an introductory lecture on his opera, illustrating it with examples played by himself at the piano, or by the orchestra and singers. He re/ peated this lecture, adjusting it as the occasions demanded, in

the towns printed above in italics. On our journey back from
Oldenburg he gave me a copy of his lecture notes. He had not
been able to deal with all the parts of the opera with equal
thoroughness, and consequently he expressly forbade that it
should be published. But when I was asked to supply a bro-
chure on the work for the American premières of *Wozzeck*
(Philadelphia and New York 1931, conductor Leopold
Stokowski) I was permitted to re-work the lecture according to
Berg's directions in such a way that all parts of the opera were
treated with equal attention (as far as possible) and the music
examples largely eliminated. In this form Berg's text is also
included in the discussion of *Wozzeck* contained in this
book.

In the spring of 1929, Ružena Herlinger, a singer from
Prague who was living in Vienna, asked Berg for a concert
aria for soprano and orchestra. Berg interrupted work on *Lulu*
and in a few months composed 'Der Wein' using texts by
Baudelaire translated into German by Stefan George. The
short score was finished on 23rd July, and the fair copy of the
full score was ready on 23rd August. That very day I visited
him in Trahütten. He was in the gayest of moods; not only
because the commission had been 'dealt with' so happily, but
also because he could now return with fresh intensity to the
opera, the musical character of which he had anticipated in
some features of the aria.

At that time I too was inspired by a tremendous spirit of
enterprise: a month before I had begun to busy myself with the
art of photography, with the audacious ulterior motive of
furnishing my future work—I was the man of letters whom Berg
had detailed to be his biographer—with photographs of my
own taking. During my stay in Trahütten I snapped away
continuously around the house and grounds with my primitive
Kodak box. The centre of my target was naturally the honoured
teacher and hero of my literary ambitions. When I got home I
sent the master my bungling efforts together with a proud letter.
I only had to wait two days and a fat letter arrived in answer.

Apart from a little note signed 'Uncle Alban' which ran as follows: 'Very praiseworthy that out of three dozen snapshots seven should have turned out so well. Bravo! Keep up the good work!' I took out of the envelope seven pencil drawings that corresponded exactly to my art-products, but caricatured their pictorial weaknesses by immeasurable exaggeration. The ridiculousness of my photographic experiments was further underlined by satirical remarks written on the reverse side of the drawings. But behind the gay derision with which Berg accepted my first photographic rapine of him and his sur-roundings—later there were to be many, many more—there is something else to be inferred from his graphic expectora-tions. They show the exactitude with which he executed every task he set himself; the fidelity with which he portrayed the original prints; and his spiritual superiority in dealing with his themes.

An epistolary discussion of certain problems of twelve-note technique that I considered parallel with geometrical con-stellations was a further result of that visit. As an example I introduced central perspective as corresponding to augmenta-tion and diminution of a motif, a technique familiar in music since the early contrapuntalists. I also wrote about 'complemen-tary series' in which it was possible—on account of their special construction—, knowing a few of the notes, to deduce the rest. He replied (in a letter of 4th September 1929) with a remark that is very revealing about his general attitude to twelve-note technique: 'How far these complementary series are musically significant is a question that I cannot decide very quickly. In any case, if you could derive from them, so that something tonal (or let's say, something of the rules of the old tonality) is in-cluded in twelve-note composition, that would be a great gain for the musical side.' Shortly afterwards (20th and 21st Sep-tember) he gave me exhaustive information about two sorts of complementary series which one could make use of 'if, in a work of several hours like an opera, one believes that a single series is not sufficient, or at least for the sake of a change'. This

remark refers directly to his work on the opera *Lulu* in which
he uses such series to a considerable extent.

The summer of 1930 brought Berg a great personal treat. His
material position had been considerably improved by royalties
from operatic and concert performances. These were steadily
increasing. The first 'luxury' he permitted himself was the purchase of a small Ford car which he loved dearly, and he
proudly sent photographs cf it to all his friends. He was soon
an excellent driver and kept a record, with characteristic exactitude, of all his driving exploits, though he never succumbed to
sporting ambitions. His afternoon drives in the summer were
his greatest relaxation after strenuous creative work. The following lines, written to Erich Kleiber on 29th October 1930
just after the latter had returned from his first conducting trip
to New York, tell of his enthusiasm for his car: 'We only
recently got back from the "country". I have brought *Lulu* a
large step forward. My "Ford" however progresses faster and
higher (60 m.p.h. and mountain roads up to 6,000 feet!).
But how high and wide will you have brought things in New
York!!!'

The contrast between the constantly growing international
recognition of Berg's work and personality and the fact that in
his homeland he was almost completely ignored, filled him
with increasing bitterness. He was no vain climber, and the
desire for honours was quite foreign to his nature. However
he was quite conscious of his artistic rank, and it pained him a
great deal if his advice was not asked when decisions were to
be made on important matters connected with Austrian music.
Wherever he did hold office—as on the executive board of the
Viennese 'Society for Authors, Composers and Music Publishers' and as a member of both executive board and jury of
the 'Allgemeinen Deutschen Musikverein' and of the 'International Society for Contemporary Music'—he did valuable
work. Honours from abroad gave him pleasure chiefly because
of the lack of recognition at home. For the same reason his
nomination on 30th January 1930 for membership of the

12   The first Wozzeck: Leo Schützendorf, baritone (Berlin 1925)

13 Berg in *c.* 1930

'Prussian Academy of Arts' was very welcome. Franz Schreker arranged that Berg was called to direct a master class in com⁄ position at the *Musikhochschule* in Berlin. Despite Schönberg's urgent pressure to accept the offer, Berg refused; he feared that his duties as an 'art official' might hinder his creative activity. He took a lively interest in all questions concerned with public musical life. He read the criticisms of his own work and that of others with an attentive and objective eye, guided by his desire to learn what he could from true representations, to put right possible errors, and expose any malevolent falsifications.

In September 1931 I had developed the idea of founding a polemical musical magazine in Vienna; Berg greeted this pro⁄ ject with joyous approval, a reaction which will hardly surprise the reader of the above description of his general attitude to music criticism. At the first mention of it he wrote to me on 12th September 1931: 'There is a real need for such a musical "torch" [analogous to the polemical magazine "Die Fackel" edited in Vienna by Karl Kraus since 1899]; I have been wishing for one for the last twenty⁄five years. What I would like best would be to write it myself; but that would mean giving up composition. But if you want to try!!! there is a great deal to be discussed. The titles you propose are all bad, I think. But I can't think of a good one either.'

After a lot of to⁄ and fro⁄ing we finally agreed on the title '23—a Viennese Music Magazine' ('23—Eine Weiner Musik⁄ zeitschrift'), a title which derived, officially, from the number of the paragraph in Austrian press law which one can call on for the correction of a newspaper article. Secretly, however, the title originated from Berg's 'fateful number' 23. Berg drew the title page, following a design by the sculptor Josef Humplik. He sent his drawing with the following remarks, which we reprint as an example of the exactitude with which he con⁄ sidered even the most trivial details: 'Enclosed is a design which I find good for the following reasons: 1. The swing of Hump⁄ lik's 23 is carried over into the word "Musikzeitschrift" and yet transformed into the rectangular. 2. The comma (23, Eine

Musikzeitschrift) seems to me to be distinctly *composed out.*
3. "Musik" is prominent—NB "Eine Wiener" and "Zeitschrift" have the same number of letters.'

The first number of the magazine appeared in January 1932,
the last one (No. 31/33) in September 1937. Owner, publisher
and responsible editor was myself. The editorial board consisted of Ernst Křenek, who was represented by contributions
in every number, Rudolf Ploderer, a solicitor and close friend
of the Bergs, and myself. Berg read every manuscript and every
galley proof and advised on all matters down to the smallest
detail of grammar. He also had a controlling finger in the
styling of the 'Justification' which introduced the first number,
and in the following passages in particular: 'We want to set
right! To set right whatever is crooked, half-baked, false,
malevolent or inimical to true values in the far-flung circles of
the arts and matters connected with the muses—the framework
is not to be too narrow. And we know that we have here a
large field for action—and one that needs to be worked over . . .
We maintain that a fruitful and profitable criticism and attack
on the ills and evils of Viennese artistic life can be carried out
for once from an independent standpoint, using above all the
means of satire and polemics . . . Day by day we see that the
task of art criticism is not carried out, indeed the arrogated
office is frequently mis-used. This is to be changed, matters
that have been concealed will be brought into the open, a new
direction will be given, things will be set right. That is why
we have chosen the paragraph of Austrian press law that deals
with correction as our *leitmotiv.*'

Berg kept a sharp critical eye on the reckless beginnings of
the magazine and made numerous suggestions for improve-
ments. He welcomed it joyfully when the magazine climbed
slowly onto a higher spiritual level and won new and important contributors. He took a passionate interest in the weari-
some libel action brought against me by the leading Viennese
music critic Julius Korngold straight after the appearance of the
first number (the action eventually ended with my acquittal).

When the court hearings were going on he never forgot to 'keep his fingers crossed' for me.

On October 1932 Berg was in a position to realize another wish that was close to his heart: the possession of his own laboratorium in the country. He bought the 'Waldhaus' situ-ated not far from Velden on the lightly populated south bank of the Wörthersee in Kärnten. From now on this was to be his favourite resort. When the Bergs took over the property it was in a completely decrepit condition, but within a short space of time Frau Helene converted it into a model of natural comfort and functional simplicity.

Generally Berg felt well and happy in his work, and the mild Kärnten climate was good for his asthma. Proudly he referred to the Waldhaus as his 'workshop' and liked to toy with the idea of settling there permanently at a later date. A summer's day at the Waldhaus ran somewhat as follows: early morning to noon, composing; then a bathe in the lake; after lunch an hour's sleep; then one or two cups of strong tea, reading the newspapers and attending to correspondence; at four o'clock a drive in the car and usually a visit to the cinema in Velden, Villach or Klagenfurt; after supper: listening to the radio and an early bed. Sometimes he would spend the after-noon too in musical work (fair copies or instrumentation). This programme enabled him to make unusually rapid progress with his creative work.

In these last 'nazi-free' years Berg's general mood was gay and confident; he could look back with satisfaction on what he and his musical friends had achieved. The speech he made in the small Musikvereinssaal in Vienna on 20th June 1932 on the occasion of the first Hertzka memorial celebration reflects this mood of gaiety and confidence.

Fourth Interlude

Ladies and Gentlemen

Of the many enemies that the living composer has, one is the publisher. Not surprising! On the one hand there is the artist, whose activity—if he is concerned with matters proper to his art—is directed towards the spiritual, and on the other hand there is the business man, whose activity—if he is concerned with matters proper to his business—is directed towards the material. I would not dare pronounce this commonplace about the gulf between artist and dealer, between idealism and realism, if we were not living in a time when this realization is hardly a commonplace any more—indeed, today the oppo-site tends to be considered obvious: the artist has to be 'matter-of-fact' . . . since in any case . . . the dealer is 'inspired'.

So if I am to persist in my view of the ideal artist who stands in contrast to the realities of the world, I will have to cast my glance back—and this quarter century of Universal Edition makes it possible for me to do so—to a time when this view was not yet antiquated, and when this contrast was considered a sheer and unbridgeable gulf. A back-glance over twenty or thirty years is sufficient—nay, a glance at the programme of today's memorial celebration programme is sufficient, with the three composers Bruckner, Mahler and Schönberg united in a single concert. To us today that seems quite natural; in those days it was daring to perform even one work by one of them.

Do you recall, ladies and gentlemen, the scenes that occurred in this very building when such music was performed? Even Bruckner—who had been dead some years—was a long way from being 'generally recognized' or 'arrived' as one calls it. Societies had to be founded to bring his work within reach of the world's understanding. These societies considered it their business to make propaganda, as we call it today: introductory lectures, and performances of his symphonies in four-hand piano reductions—I was present at such meetings in this very room—all this was necessary for Bruckner at that time. Even his pupils and those who were considered the composer's closest friends saw fit to touch up his works and make extensive 'cuts', i.e.—so as to make the works palatable for the musical world at all—to mutilate them.

So if at that time the cultivation of Bruckner's music was the internal affair of societies (that bore his name or Wagner's or Hugo Wolf's . . .), in what state was the cultivation of the music of Mahler and Schönberg? I do not need to remind you of the scenes that took place in this building when such music was performed. Even though Mahler had found a large 'audience', the enthusiasm of this audience for this 'secessionistic' music, for this 'conductor's music' was completely incomprehensible to the musical world at large. Just as incomprehensible as the general rejection of that 'impostor' Schönberg's 'cacophonies' was comprehensible and welcome. In this case the general musical world did not stand in opposition to the efforts of a 'society' or the enthusiasm of a particular 'audience', but merely to the view of a small group of hangers-on which would only be described as the 'Schönberg clique'.

So that was the effect of what was presented to the world as new music, a quarter century ago. And the composers—and their societies, special audiences and cliques—believed in all seriousness that their works should not only be performed and heard, but also preserved for posterity, printed, published!

I must say that it is a tall order for a business man—and a publisher has to be that—to dispose of a ware that the consumer has rejected as unpalatable. Ladies and gentlemen, picture this and keep in your mind's eye the discrepancy between these two spheres of interest, and you will not accuse me of having

exaggerated when I spoke at the outset about a 'sheer, unbridgeable gulf' between artist and dealer, and of the 'enmity'
that must appear when two such worlds come face to face.

And yet! the thing that could not be expected, that contradicts all calculating logic and all business usage—happened!
A business man appeared who was prepared to range himself
on the side of the economically weaker party—and the party
which had never been right—in the apparently hopeless battle
between producer and consumer! For what could a little heap
of musicians signify compared with the World Power of
recognized music? What difference would it make if a couple
of publicity helpers joined forces with the dozen (at most)
young composers? And what if a couple of performances *did*
create 'sensations'—i.e. tot up a spiritual *plus* which could not
possibly blind anyone to the *minus* of the general deficit. What
can be going on in the brain of a business man (and one who
understood his business as it turned out later) to make him
decide in favour of such a thing—a thing that could not
redound to his credit nor lead to material success; a thing, consequently, that no other publisher in the world wanted to have
anything to do with. What can be going on in a business man's
brain that he ever recognizes these few musical events as the
beginning of a movement—a movement that would last for
twenty-five years, and remains today the only movement of
which one can say that it is still a movement. And finally we
must ask ourselves: what power had this small business man—
which is what he was at the time—at his disposal, that he could
convert his fantastic knowledge into plans, and convert these
in turn into action, and then in the course of a quarter century
communicate this irresistibly to the whole musical world,
literally to force it on the public?

We know that it was not one of those powers that almost
everything can be traced back to when great and successful
undertakings are called into being—even those of a spiritual
nature—that is, it was not the power of money nor yet that of
position. Nor was it one of those power-factors that are essential

to the successful achievement of anything in Vienna—the power-factors of the press, of Viennese Society 'insofar as they are possessed of rank and name' and have 'connections' with the 'heads of authority, art and science'.

So what power was it that accomplished something here that otherwise seems unthinkable without the collaboration of these factors?

I have no other answer—and for us musicians there is no other explanation—than: it was the power of the idea! The idea that was brought into the world with the 'musical move-ment' that I was speaking of earlier; the idea from which the whole spiritual debit and credit of this publishing house derives, even the material success which in the end was not lacking, even the real power that went out from this publishing house, and the leading position that it occupies today. So that it will not surprise you, ladies and gentlemen—nor the non-musicians amongst you—when I maintain that the spiritual concept that proceeds from the words 'Universal Edition' plays a far more important part in the imagination of us composers than the fact that it is also the name of such a well-conducted, brilliantly organized, and consequently successful publishing business. And you will not be surprised when I further main-tain—accepting the danger that it may sound paradoxical—that it does not really depend so much on the things that are usually extolled when a great publisher dies, such as: that the works of several hundred composers are published, and that in the course of a quarter century of publishing work the number of their works is raised from 2,000 to 10,000,

that the work of the publisher extends over all the diverse fields of music,

that, just as the musical movement of this time is not limited to Vienna, where it originated, nor to Germany, where it quickly spread, but has become a universal one . . ., so the publishing house too, faithful to its name, showed a univer-sality that extended over the whole of the musical world. This almost suggests the idea at the present festival of the International

Society for Contemporary Music that this publishing house should be honoured with the title 'Internation Limited Com, pany for Contemporary Music',

and that finally, there was no lack of what is necessary for ensuring the international standing of a publisher, i.e. the success of the published authors in all gradations: beginning with the momentary success of local greatness, and ending with the glory of famous names that will outlast the present time and take their places in eternity.

And despite this, however characteristic and important the matters indicated here may be for the assessment of a publishing house, . . . despite this I would like to say that all these matters —which are preserved better and with more completeness than I can bring to the task in the catalogues and annual reports and the other business papers of this Limited Company—all these matters seem to me to be the private concern of the authors— and stockholders. But what has been written down in the course of this quarter century on five-line paper is no private concern, but the concern of the history of music. And it is alive, just as it was twenty-five years ago, because it serves the idea of that great musical movement—and in the end it must be right, for this spiritual capital is perhaps the only kind of capital that is not subject to the risk of a crisis. It cannot be devalued.

That, at least, is how I see the situation of music today and tomorrow, and the situation of Universal Edition is inextricably bound up with it. And I think I have spoken on behalf of all the Edition's composers.

I was asked to speak 'in their name', and what I have said so far has been intended in this way. But if I have hitherto hardly spoken about the man who was—I can find no more honourable description—the bearer, the agent, the custodian of that 'idea', I have refrained because it would have meant lapsing from the general onto the personal level. And if I were to do that, if I were to speak of what is close to my own heart, then I would become too personal. My speech—which is

14 At the window of his Vienna home, *c.* 1932. In front of him is his portrait, painted by Arnold Schönberg in 1920.

15 *(above)* Berg and his wife in their Vienna home. On the right is the American soprano, Anne Roselle. 16 *(below)* With Hans Rosbaud at the first 'Maggio Musicale Fiorentino', 1933

17 (*above*) In Lucca, May, 1933. 18 (*below*) With his wife and Frau Erna Apostel in front of the Waldhaus, April, 1934

19   In the Vienna studio of the Swiss artist, Franz Rederer, 1934

supposed to be filled with the radiant recognition of that 'idea' —would then bear a dark tone of profound sadness, which I wanted to avoid, for what brings us together here today is no mourning ceremony but a memorial feast, one that is to be repeated every year, that is, it extends forwards to a time when our joy in the possession of the idea left by this extraordinary man is no longer darkened by the pain we suffer at his loss. When that time comes we will know—and here again I am speaking on behalf of all—that my initial proposition about the enmity between composer and publisher, although proved by historical facts, cannot be asserted in this—perhaps unique— case. For:

Of the few friends that we living composers have, this was one, our publisher Emil Hertzka.

This speech was made on 20th June 1932 in the small Musikvereinssaal in Vienna on the occasion of the first Hertzka memorial celebration

THE LAST YEARS

The purchase of the Waldhaus had stretched Berg's financial position to the utmost, and when Hitlerism came to power in Germany at the end of January 1933 it had a catastrophic effect. Had the position remained as it was before, Berg could have reckoned on covering his cost of living without any trouble; the income from his opera and concert performances had been steadily increasing and Universal Edition had been giving him a monthly retainer until the completion of *Lulu* (an advance against future royalties). But the changes in Germany had nothing but an unfavourable effect on his material position. The National Socialists (Nazis) regarded all the music of Schönberg's school as 'degenerate art'; *Wozzeck* could not be performed any more in Germany. Theatres that had already contracted for the work annulled their contracts, and even in German concerts his works could no longer be performed. Berg was very exact and far-sighted in material matters as in all things, and this deterioration of his position confounded him completely. Unremittingly he tried to think of possible means of raising his income. Above all he increased his speed of work more and more. He wanted to complete *Lulu* as fast as possible so as to obtain the money that would come from the planned performances abroad. From this moment on he was granted only a few short periods of respite and relaxation.

He enjoyed one such period in Florence at the beginning of May. He was a guest of honour at the music congress held on the occasion of the first 'Maggio Musicale Fiorentino' and he was celebrated both by his hosts and by the international public. I was constantly at his side as his travel-manager and interpreter

and there were days of cloudless gaiety. With the utmost conscientiousness he visited all the meetings of the congress, and
even the most boring of them was a source of purest pleasure
when one could watch how he sketched on the back of the
resumé of the congressional speeches: he took great care over
his lightly caricatured portraits of the speakers and was very
indignant if a speaker stopped speaking before he had put the
finishing touches—in colour—to his picture. Our meals together were another thing I shall never forget: he insisted on
trying out, with childish inquisitiveness, all the dishes he did
not know on the Italian menu, and refused to be discouraged by
his frequent bitter disappointments. His meeting with Carl
Ebert was very stimulating for him artistically; of all operatic
directors he had the highest opinion of Ebert, and would dearly
have liked to entrust the première of *Lulu* to him.

In the middle of May he took up work on the opera with
redoubled intensity at the Waldhaus. At the same time he
watched with dismay and sadness the developments in Germany, and the fact that the Austrian attitude to the radical
new art hardly differed from the one current in Germany filled
him with intolerable bitterness. On 3rd November 1933 he
wrote to me of the enthusiastic reception accorded to Schönberg
on his arrival in New York: 'There is really nothing for
Vienna to be proud of in the fact that Schönberg was driven
out of Berlin. There he is only *one* of the *many* victims. . . . But
Austria, at a time when the Walters and Hubermänner are just
being celebrated and made into martyrs, has treated Schönberg
as dirtily as ever. That's why we must rub their noses in it and
point to the way America behaves towards Schönberg. It is not
enough that one knows—from the newspapers, etc,—that
Schönberg is one of the hundred Jewish artists who have fled
to America, one has to make plain that what has long been
due has now happened, because Schönberg is *free*. That it was
long overdue is proved by the various teaching posts offered
him, and the concerts etc, all spoken about in that *first* article
in "Musical America". And now point to Vienna: where are

the teaching posts for the Austrian Arnold Schönberg, where are the concerts and receptions, etc, and what is being dissemi′ nated and performed *instead* . . . Then take up again the com′ plex of thoughts about the article "Which Camp is Austria in?" which I suggested to you before, but which could not be taken into account. And since in the policy of "23" you apparently have to soft′pedal on Germany (on account of the artists who are still there) your main avenue of attack must be the Austrian problem . . .'

To accelerate the completion of the opera Berg decided in the autumn of 1933 not to return to Vienna as was his habit, but to stay and spend the winter in the Waldhaus. One can get an idea of what wintering in the Waldhaus meant from a letter he sent to Schönberg in America on 9th December 1933. In the rough draft he writes, among other things: 'So we are really still here in this wilderness, surrounded by snow and ice for the last two months. Besides my [one word illegible] work on *Lulu*, we are encumbered with all the small and petty wor′ ries of such a sojourn, as for instance (to restrict myself to a couple of things which may serve to illustrate the contrast be′ tween your life and ours): Which farmer sells the dryest wood, or whether or no the pipes are going to freeze tonight, or shall we risk a little trip in the car to Klagenfurt or Velden for the pleasure of a warm bath, etc. Having given you a hint of all this, yet repeating once more that I would still rather be here than in Vienna for only thus can I find the concentration for composing, you will not be surprised that we describe our self′ inflicted exile as a "concentration camp" . . .'

In the same letter he asked whether Schönberg could help him sell the three′volume original manuscript of the score of *Wozzeck*. And Schönberg actually did succeed in persuading the Library of Congress in Washington to buy the manuscript. Berg's material worries were slightly alleviated by the prospect of this money, and it also seems to have had a favourable effect on the progress of his work. For on 6th May he could write to Webern: 'Writing the full′stop at the end of the composition of *Lulu* has not made my happiness as complete as one might have imagined. Just in the penultimate part I have only fleet/ ingly sketched some things and postponed the execution of them until later. And besides, I now have to "overhaul" (as one says of a car) the whole composition from the beginning! A work that stretches over years and a musical development that is not *quite* completely surveyable right from the start forces one to look back over it, and there will be things that have to be touched up. This will all take another two or three weeks, so I can only start on the instrumentation in June . . . and the time available (till the autumn!) gets shorter and shorter—and with it my nervousness—gets longer and longer.'

The autumn dead/line was dictated by Berg's urgent desire to have the opera ready for performance in the 1934/35 season. He was thinking of a première in the Berlin State Opera under the direction of Erich Kleiber. At Kleiber's suggestion he cor/ responded with Wilhelm Furtwängler on the subject, and also with the general superintendent Heinz Tietjen. As 'privy councillor' Furtwängler had a lot of influence in musical matters at that time. But on 29th May Berg wrote to Kleiber: 'My dear friend, the die is cast. I have just received a letter from Furtwängler (a very charming one, incidentally) which makes it plain that in view of the "seriousness of the present situation" there is no question of the work's being accepted for performance in Germany. Although he knows (and "one" knows) that I am a German composer and an Aryan and also that Wedekind is a German and an Aryan. Now I would like to inform you of the following: I am now making a suite out of *Lulu* which will last approximately twenty/five minutes. UE wants to publish it as soon as possible so that in the autumn all the orchestral societies (in the world!) can play it. Naturally they are thinking primarily of you. Do you have the desire and the opportunity and the courage to make the first performance?'

Kleiber joyfully accepted straight away and gave the première of the 'suite' (Five Symphonic Pieces from the Opera Lulu) on the scheduled date (30th November 1934) in a concert of the Berlin *Staatskapelle* in the opera house *Unter den Linden,* despite mighty external difficulties. We will speak of this 'dramatic' event in detail at the proper time. First we have to consider two matters that beset Berg after he had finished the instrumentation of the Lulu Symphony in July.

For Schönberg's sixtieth birthday (13th September 1934) Universal Edition planned a publication in his honour, and Webern had taken over the editorship. Berg contributed an ingeniously constructed acrostic poem which places the three Christian cardinal virtues—faith, hope and love—in intimate relationship with Schönberg's activity in general and with Berg's personal experiences with the master. Further he took a lively interest in my modest prose contribution ('Plea of the Younger Ones') and subjected my first draft to severe criticism (5th August) which I reproduce here word for word because it contains important statements of principle concerning Berg's attitude to twelve-note music. In the letter he says: 'Your article is very beautifully written and not at all conventional. [This opening is typical of the kindliness of Berg's pedagogic method. W.R.] But in my view it cannot stand as it is. The central passage which I have crossed out cannot be included. Apart from the quoted phrases that will not be understood— "the adventures of work" (Karl Kraus); one has to know where the phrase comes from and how it is to be understood— well, that is not so serious, but that about the "private concern" refers only to the *purely technical* aspect of twelve-note music (which is indeed the private concern of each composer, just as the utilization of tonality was); but Schönberg would cer-tainly not wish *the work itself* to be regarded as his private concern. That would make a meal for his opponents! And the interpretation called forth by your middle sentence would be just as much of a meal for anyone who wanted to trip Schön-berg up: "Aha! So *nobody* understands his music except the very close associates who have worked with him for twenty or thirty years. The spiritual atmosphere of his most recent works is not accessible even for the younger adherents with the best will in the world, and they are even less performable than the earlier works (acoustic realization gets less and less). If someone who is right in the clique says that then it's probably right, which makes it that much easier for us to ignore his private concerns on his sixtieth birthday!" So that bit cannot be left in! Yes, but what to put in its place and still reach your final conclusion? Perhaps just the opposite: the younger ones recognize more and more that *this* is the way of music (and always has been); music (as in Karl Kraus's poem) does not emerge from a state of "ecstatic intoxication" as the dilettante imagines, but from the *ecstasies of logic* (twelve-note system,) etc. etc. So good luck with the repairs! You'll succeed all right, because what you say *in the main* is perfectly right and is also said *very beautifully*.' Naturally I followed Berg's advice, and had the satisfaction of knowing that the final version of my article was completely acceptable to him, and also to Schönberg.

The second matter which interrupted his work that summer was concerned with his involvement in the music festival organized in connection with the Venice 'Biennale' in September. He had been placed on the committee of honour on the basis of the success achieved by his music the previous year in Italy (Lyric Suite and *Wozzeck* fragments). And the *Wozzeck* pieces had been put in the programme of concerts. At the beginning of July he heard that his name had been struck off the committee list and his work removed from the programme. He rightly guessed that these measures had been taken as a result of National Socialist machinations, and he made an energetic protest through his friends the Italian composers Gian Francesco Malipiero and Alfredo Casella. The result: his name was put back on the committee list and his aria 'Der Wein' was performed for the first time in Italy in the third festival concert on 11th September in the Teatro Fenice. Under Hermann Scherchen's bâton, and despite insufficient rehearsal time, the work was greeted with enthusiasm by the audience. Berg was present in person—this was to be his last trip abroad —and was celebrated with great vivacity. The reviews were

also generally favourable, with the exception of the National
Socialist newspapers. This fact persuaded Berg to write the
following letter on 10th October to one of the most active of
the German critics; the letter is characteristic of the modest and
yet superior way Berg handled such matters. It runs:

'*Sehr geehrter Herr Doktor,* it is against my usual habit to
react to a "bad criticism"; even against my conviction, for I
cannot expect—indeed I do not expect—my music to please
everybody. I am making an exception in the present case for the
following reason only: Your review of the music festival in
Venice—printed in one or two dozen newspapers—contains
the sentence: "The music (of my aria 'Der Wein') circumvents
[ignores] utterly the content of the Stefan George/Baudelaire
texts." I found this sentence—couched in the same words—
over and over again in other reviews that were different in
other respects and even signed with other names, and so I was
forced to the conclusion that now thousands—even ten or a
hundred thousand—of your readers have accepted your statement as a fact. Involuntarily my interest in the originator of
such a statement presented as a fact was aroused. This may
explain, *sehr geehrter Herr* (naturally I do not take it amiss that
you consider my aria, "despite certain merits", a "monstrous"
work), my polite request that you tell me in what way my
music, which I composed for these wonderful texts and with
every intention of doing justice to them—in what way my
music circumvents the content of these texts, circumvents it
"utterly". In answering this question perhaps you would consider me, *Herr Doktor,* not as the author of this music, and a
subjectively interested party in whom you might wrongly sus-
pect the presence of a plaintive feeling of injustice, but as one
of your many, quite objective readers who is simply interested
in a more explicit substantiation of the utter circum-composi-
tion that you assert. In the pleasant anticipation that you will
not deny me the fulfilment of my request, I sign myself, with
the highest respect . . .' It is surely unnecessary for me to mention that this letter never received an answer.

The incidents preceding the Venice music festival and this one-sided polemical letter were symptoms of the critical situa/ tion that surrounded Berg in Germany—a situation that be/ came gradually more critical with the approach of the Berlin première of the Lulu Symphony. However, some artistic com/ ment on the new work was required for the programme book/ let and it fell to me to provide this, with Berg's collaboration. I also had the honour of representing him at the concert and in the final rehearsals; at that time he did not feel at all well physically and wished to avoid the exertions of the journey and all the excitement that would surely have accompanied his stay in Berlin. The boldness of Kleiber's undertaking is indicated by the fact that the authorities—at his request—were willing to guarantee that there would be no disturbance during the con/ cert but they were not prepared to offer protection should demonstrations arise later.

After some wonderful hours of intensive musical preparation with Kleiber and his orchestra, the memorable première took place on 30th November 1934. The Lulu Symphony was received with loud applause; this also revealed the disapproval of the régime's cultural policy. Only *one* opposing voice was heard: a man—a visiting Viennese into the bargain—ran through the stalls roaring 'Hail Mozart!' Kleiber turned to him and answered, 'You have made a mistake, the piece is by Alban Berg.' The next day the Berlin newspapers carried violent attacks on the work and the performance. One said that the music was fully worthy of Wedekind's play, it heaped scandal on scandal and could hardly be of interest to the German people. Abroad, the Lulu Symphony was performed more than ten times in the following months. Four days after the concert Kleiber resigned from his position of General Musical Director in Berlin and left Germany at the beginning of 1935.

Berg, who was back in Vienna since the end of October 1934, suffered unspeakably under the deterioration of the cul/ tural situation in Austria. So he welcomed with enthusiasm

the proposed foundation—at Schönberg's instigation—of a
spiritual 'defensive alliance' (it never came into being). On
30th January he writes: 'You would never believe—or no,—
you do have a notion how necessary that is for us Austrians.
Our art—which is not considered indigenous—and therefore our
whole material existence is just as much threatened here as in
other places where "cultural bolshevism" is being expressly
persecuted, and one thinks and talks of nothing but how one
can oppose this attitude. Unfortunately one is very handicapped
in this by the fact that at the moment we can do practically
nothing without the opposition mixing it up with political
matters, which is just what we do not want (and never have
wanted). So it is all the more necessary for us "threatened ones"
to work out some such spiritual alliance of an unpolitical
nature.'

This quotation shows unmistakably what sort of mood
dominated Berg at the beginning of the last year of his life.
Even the numerous honours that fell to him on his fiftieth
birthday (9th February 1935)—musical celebrations, appreciations in the press and personal presents—could not wrench
him out of this mood. A short time afterwards, on 27th February, he sent a reproduction of an old Viennese engraving to
the widow of Director Hertzka at her Viennese home '*am
Kaasgraben*' where he had been a guest the day before. The
engraving shows part of the street 'Tuchlauben' in the 'Inner
town' and Berg's accompanying letter ran: 'On this picture
you can see: 1. on the right, the shop where the seventh Beethoven symphony was published in 1812, an edition which is
in my possession since yesterday's beautiful, so-comfortable
evening in the Kaasgraben. A hundred years later my Opus 1
was published in the same house. 2. On the top floor of the
same house on the right are the rooms where this Opus 1 was
first performed (in Director Hertzka's *Tonkünstler* Society),
and it was repeated *in the same spot* (in the ladies' club) twenty-
five years later on the occasion of my fiftieth birthday. 3. The
house in the centre, finally, is the house where—on 9th

February 1885—I was born. And since, despite fifty years living and working in my fatherland, I am still not found "indigenous", I have answered a questionnaire—sent round by the "Echo"—on the subject of Handel and Bach, who have just reached the age of 250, as follows: "What luck that Handel and Bach were born in the year 1685 and not 200 years later! If they had been, there would have been questions about whether the one was 'indigenous' to his fatherland, and the music of the other would have been considered cultural bolshevism. I am ready and willing to demonstrate this. Alban Berg." Plainly enough, my reply—so urgently requested by the paper—was not published after all, and the "Echo" made do with answers from state, court and government officials and professors. And since I have not managed to achieve even the lastmentioned rank, I do not even have the right to be so forgetful as to leave my umbrella in the beautiful, socomfortable house *am Kaasgraben* . . .'

As Berg was writing these lines so saturated with melancholic irony, he was already thinking intensively about a new work, for the sake of which he even wanted to interrupt his work on the instrumentation of *Lulu*. Shortly before he had been commissioned by the American violinist Louis Krasner to write a Violin Concerto. Following this he occupied himself unceasingly with the project, but could not make up his mind about what form the work should have. However, on 28th March he could write to Krasner: 'With joy, I hear that you want to stay and work in Europe for the summer. From May on I will be on the Wörthersee (diagonally opposite Pörtschach, where Brahms' Violin Concerto was written) composing "our" Violin Concerto, so perhaps we can keep in touch with one another while the work is being written.'

Shortly afterwards a catastrophic happening triggered the decisive creative impulse: Manon Gropius, whom the Bergs loved dearly, the nineteenyearold, wonderfully beautiful daughter of Alma Maria Mahler, died suddenly on 22nd April of a paralysis of the central nervous system—an aftereffect

of the infantile paralysis which had attacked her a year before
and which she had suffered with gay composure. A few days
later Berg was in his Waldhaus composing his Violin Concerto at a feverish tempo unknown to him before. On 23rd July
he finished the short score, and on 11th August the fair copy of
the full score was ready. He dedicated the work 'to the memory
of an angel'. In the first part Berg—as he said himself—sought
to translate features of the young girl's character into musical
terms, while the second part falls clearly into the framework of
Catastrophe and Resolution. The resolution is effected by
means of a Bach chorale (from the Cantata 'O Ewigkeit, du
Donnerwort' written in 1732). The words to this chorale are:

> *Es ist genug!—*
> *Herr, wenn es dir gefällt,*
> *So spanne mich doch aus!*
> *Mein Jesus kommt:*
> *Nun gute Nacht, o Welt!*
> *Ich fahr' ins Himmelshaus,*
> *Ich fahre sicher hin mit Frieden,*
> *Mein grosser Jammer bleibt darnieden.*
> *Es ist genug! es ist genug!*

(It is enough! Lord, if it is thy pleasure, relieve me of my yoke!
My Jesus cometh: now good night, O world! I am going up into
the house of heaven, surely am I going there in peace; my great
distress remains below. It is enough, it is enough!)

This places the work in a remarkably close relationship with
the last works of Bach and Brahms, which were also dominated
by chorales whose texts were just as rich in references. The profound significance that the series of notes to the words 'Es ist
genug' came to have for the whole concerto—in the way they
are introduced and manipulated—is surely a kind of internal
evidence that Berg planned the work with the vague premoni-
tion that it was to be his own requiem.

The following quotations from letters written to me in June
and July 1935 are specially important with regard to the story of
how the Violin Concerto came into being because they prove
—as opposed to the assertion that is sometimes made that Berg

had taken the Bach chorale as a basis for the composition of the concerto from the start—that the idea of introducing the chorale only crystallized in Berg's mind when the composition was already quite advanced. After informing me on 7th June of the rapid progress of his work, he wrote to me the next day: 'Please send me (on loan) the St Matthew Passion (full or vocal score) and, if you own one, a collection of chorales (I need a chorale melody for my work—discretion!)' When I visited him in the Waldhaus a week later he showed me—in the collection I had sent him: '60 Choralgesänge von Johann Sebastian Bach' (selected and introduced by Herman Roth, published by Drei Masken Verlag, Munich 1920—the chorale selected by Berg bears the number 55)—the chorale 'Es ist genug! . . .' and said 'Isn't that remarkable: the first four notes of the chorale (a series of whole tones) correspond exactly to the last four notes of the twelve-note series on which I am constructing the whole concerto?' And on 1st July he wrote to me: 'I hope to be ready with the composition by the middle of July, and have the score ready in time for the Karlsbad Music Festival. I am *hoping*—so please touch wood three times! Now I beg you: please write out the *text* of the chorale "Es ist genug! So nimm, Herr, meinen Geist" ("It is enough! So take, Lord, my spirit") from your little chorale book for me. I forgot it. (Only the text!) *I* wrote out the music.'

On my next visit to the Waldhaus (10th and 11th August) Berg played through the whole of the Violin Concerto with me as a piano duet. Highly pleased by the unexpectedly rapid completion of the work he told me about the projects that he wished to take up after he had dealt with the instrumentation of *Lulu*. He was thinking of a third string quartet, a piece of chamber music with piano, a symphony, a work to be written specially for radio, and above all a work for sound-film, a field that had always interested him because of the new artistic possibilities it offered. He also spoke of his pet idea of having *Wozzeck* filmed with a picked ensemble of actors and singers; he pointed out how the formal arrangement of his first opera corresponded almost exactly to the technique of film, and that a film would be able to realize certain details to perfection by means of close-ups and long shots (as an example he cited the street scene in Act II—fantasia and fugue with three themes)—details that never emerged with the desired clarity in the theatre.

On this visit we also discussed our plan to publish an analysis that I had made of the Violin Concerto in a Viennese daily newspaper on 31st August, Mrs Mahler's birthday. The plan was successful and on 1st September Berg wrote to me: 'Even before I had had a chance to read the article I received a telegram worded as follows: "Only-beloved people! With this enormous deed of love you have made me the only birthday present that could give me joy. My yearning for you both is insupportable. Alban, I kiss your blessed hand, and Helene, your dear mouth. Eternally and ever your Alma." Naturally I was very very pleased. We have hit on the right decision once again! Thanks to you too, dear friend!'

In the first days of September Berg was supposed to take part in the ISCM festival as the delegate of the Viennese section of the Society. The festival had been moved from Karlsbad to Prague; among other things, the programme listed a perfor-mance of the Lulu Symphony. But at the last moment he was not able to go, because he had incurred—from an insect sting, as he thought—an abscess on his back. He had mentioned it to me in the middle of August: 'For the rest, my pleasure in the liberation following the completion of the Violin Concerto was premature. An insect sting exactly at the lower end of the backbone led—a crescendo lasting days—to a frightfully pain-ful abscess that takes away all my pleasure. At the moment it seems to be subsiding, but it will probably take another week. So I continue in a resigned frame of mind with the instrumen-tation of *Lulu*.' The abscess was treated surgically and healed for the time being; but this may well have been the beginning of his fatal illness.

The last letter I received from him (4th November) tells of the severe worry caused him by his financial emergency and his physical pain. He wrote: 'For somehow or other we *must* be helped! And this cry is one of the main reasons for my coming to Vienna. *I can live for one, two months more*—but what then? I am thinking and working out combinations of nothing except this—so I am profoundly depressed. My health is also somewhat below par, but the pain has abated to more moderate dimensions.'

On 12th November Berg returned to Vienna in a bad condition. Large doses of aspirin, which he had been taking secretly for some weeks, kept him on his feet. In his last letter to Schönberg (30th November) he speaks with enthusiasm of the latter's *Gurrelieder* and George songs which he had just heard in Vienna, and he also expressed his satisfaction at the numerous performances of the Lulu Symphony abroad. But then he continues: 'But despite all this, things are not going well for me. Badly in a *monetary* connection, because I cannot maintain my previous standard of living, inclusive of the Waldhaus (yet I cannot make up my mind to sell the place where in two years I did *more* work than in the previous ten). Badly as regards my *health*, because for months I have been having boils (I've still got them, which explains my horizontal position!). They began shortly after I had finished the con⁄ certo with an atrocious carbuncle resulting from an insect sting. This put paid to any possibility of an autumn recupera⁄ tion period—which I rather needed after the summer's hard work and the preceding *Lulu* years. Finally things are bad *morally*, which won't astonish you coming from someone who suddenly discovers that he is not "indigenous" to his father⁄ land, and is consequently completely homeless. All heightened by the fact that such things do not proceed without friction and profound human disappointments—and these persist. But it is not for me to tell *you* such things, since you have been through it all on a gigantic scale, by comparison with which my ex⁄ periences are pocket⁄sized. After all, I still live in my native land, and can speak my mother tongue. . . .'

Feverish and run down though he was, Berg could still have a hand in the preparation of the Viennese première of the Lulu

Symphony, which took place satisfactorily on 11th December. This was the first time that he heard music from *Lulu* in the flesh—and it was to be the last time that any music reached his ears. On 14th December, in severe pain, he looked through the piano score of the Violin Concerto with Mrs Rita Kurzmann (who had made the reduction). On the 16th the pains suddenly subsided; apparently the abscess had broken open inwards, causing general blood poisoning.

On 17th December Berg was taken to the Rudolf hospital (Vienna III) and operated on immediately. The suppurative focus could not be located, neither at this stage nor in the second operation nor in the section. A blood transfusion on 19th December brought only temporary relief. Berg was either not fully aware of the seriousness of his condition, or else wanted—this is more probable—to keep it from his wife and friends; at any rate he bore the suffering with inconceivable patience and good humour. He asked to see the blood donor so as to thank him personally. He turned out to be an unconcerned young Viennese, and when he had left Berg turned to me and said, with indescribable expression: 'If only I don't turn into a composer of operetta now!'

After two days had passed comparatively well, the balance tipped towards catastrophe on 22nd December; the heart, fortified during the whole illness by the most energetic means available, failed; the doctors gave the patient up, and the last struggle began. The next morning, in all calmness, Berg asserted 'Today is the 23rd. It will be a decisive day!' In his delirium he was preoccupied with his unfinished opera; he made slight conducting motions and called out several times 'An up-beat! an up-beat!' He died on 24th December at fifteen minutes past one in the morning. A peaceful, mild expression soon effaced the traces of his frightful suffering. The death mask taken the same morning by Anna Mahler, daughter of Gustav Mahler, shows the image of a man recovered.

On 28th December in the early afternoon Berg was buried in the Hietzing cemetery in a grave endowed by the Munici-

pality of Vienna, in the presence of all Viennese circles interested in the arts. The special number of '23' dedicated to his
memory (No. 24/25, 1st February 1936) opened with an
obituary written by myself. It contained the following sentences: 'Alban Berg, our beloved master and friend deserves
every one of the following words. There is surely no need to
justify the words themselves, but the fact that we utter them
now, so soon after the catastrophe, at a time when many of us
are still numbed into silent solitude by the pain of this terrible
event—this fact needs some explanation. We draw our justification for speaking now about Alban Berg from the content of
our words and from the general and constant bond that united
this magazine with the living Alban Berg, for this volume is
consecrated to the memory of the living Alban Berg, and will
speak only of him. What we have to call after him is something
he heard even in his lifetime: Thanks, thousandfold thanks for
every moment lived with us and for us, for every smile of his
bright yet still so puzzling countenance, for every note of his
inconceivably intense and inspired work!'

Part II The Work

EARLY WORKS

The list given me by Watznauer and revised by Berg contains 90 songs (88 solo songs and two duets). Thirty-five of these were written between the summer of 1901 and the autumn of 1904, before Berg began taking lessons from Schönberg. The remaining fifty-five were composed between the winter of 1904 and the summer of 1908 during his period of study with Schönberg. There seems little point in listing all these pieces individually here; above all they are characteristic of the fervour of the young composer's world of feeling, as well as the range of his literary culture. The songs that Berg himself published and those which were published after his death are sufficient testimony to the musical bearing of the composer at this time. These are listed below with their dates of composition and first publication.

'Im Zimmer' (text by Johannes Schlaf); composed in the summer of 1905; Watznauer No. 54; published as No. 5 of the Seven Early Songs (1928).

'Liebesode' (Otto Erich Hartleben); composed in the autumn of 1906; Watznauer No. 69; published as No. 6 of the Seven Early Songs (1928).

'Die Nachtigall' (Theodor Storm); composed in the spring of 1907; Watznauer No. 76; published as No. 3 of the Seven Early Songs (1928).

'Traumgekrönt' (Rainer Maria Rilke); composed August 1907; Watznauer No. 78; published as No. 4 of the Seven Early Songs (1928).

'Schliesse mir die Augen beide . . .' (Theodor Storm); composed September 1907; Watznauer No. 80 (setting in C

An Leukon
Gleim 1764

komponiert 1908

Ro - sen pflük-ke, Ro - sen blühn, Mor - gen ist nicht

heut!_____ Kei - ne Stun - de laß ent - fliehn,___

Mit Rhythmus

Flüch - tig ist die Zeit! Trink und küs - se:

Sieh, es ist heut Ge - le - gen-heit; Weißt du, wo du

major; published from a facsimile corrected by Berg's own hand in February 1930 in the Berlin magazine 'Die Musik' (together with the second setting of the same poem composed in the twelve-note method in 1925), as a musical illustration for an article by me about Berg (*see pages* 74–75).

'Nacht' (Carl Hauptmann) and 'Schilflied' (Nikolaus Lenau); composed in the spring of 1908; Watznauer Nos. 81 and 82; published as Nos. 1 and 2 of the *Seven Early Songs* (1928).

'An Leukon' (Johann Wilhelm Ludwig Gleim); composed in the spring of 1908; Watznauer No. 84; published as a musical illustration in my book 'Alban Berg', Vienna 1937, and again here on *pages* 110–111.

'Sommertage' (Paul Hohenberg); composed in the summer of 1908; Watznauer No. 85; published as No. 7 of the *Seven Early Songs* (1928).

Four Songs to Poems by Hebbel and Mombert; composed in the summer of 1908; Watznauer Nos. 87–90; published as 'Opus 2', Berlin 1910.

The following works were also written during his student period (apart from the compositions intended solely for his lessons):

'Double Fugue for String Quintet with Piano Accompaniment (in the manner of a written-out continuo)'; composed in 1907, manuscript lost.

Twelve Variations on an Original Theme, for piano; composed 1908; published in facsimile in the book by H. F. Redlich, 'Alban Berg. Versuch einer Würdigung', Vienna 1957

Sonata for Piano; completed in the summer of 1908; published as 'Opus 1', Berlin 1910.

String Quartet, Opus 3; completed in the spring of 1910, published in Vienna 1920.

Berg's 'aphoristic epoch' directly following his period of study with Schönberg produced the following works:

Five Orchestral Songs to Postcard Texts by Peter Altenberg, Opus 4; completed in August 1912; published in Vienna, 1953 (previous publication of a piano score of the fifth song in the Dresden magazine 'Menschen', 1921—see *page 53*).

Four Pieces for Clarinet and Piano, Opus 5; composed in the summer of 1913; published in Vienna, 1920.

THREE ORCHESTRAL PIECES, OPUS 6

The circumstances concerning the composition of the work (the fair copy of the full score was completed on 23rd August 1914) and the première of Nos. 1 and 2 are given on *pages* 42 and 56–57. The première of the whole cycle with the changes of instrumentation undertaken in 1929 took place in Oldenburg on 14th April 1930. The conductor was Johannes Schüler, who one year previously had won Berg's complete confidence with his so carefully prepared Oldenburg première of *Wozzeck*. I will now quote a few sentences from a letter that Berg wrote to Schüler on 17th April 1929 a few weeks after the memorable Oldenburg première of *Wozzeck*: 'I am uncommonly pleased that you intend to perform my Three Orchestral Pieces. Surely you will be able to rehearse this difficult score in the same way as the *Wozzeck* score. That is an unconditional necessity if these pieces—at last—are to make a convincing show. Which is the reason I have held them back for so long. A performance of these orchestral pieces, which though short are very difficult, is an impossible matter in the usual concert procedure, where a number like this has to be rehearsed together with a symphony, a concerto and an overture or orchestral songs—all in two rehearsals; so I do everything I can to prevent it. . . . It has long been my intention to retouch this rather "thickly" instru﹅mentated score, but that won't change the *composition*. And since the first two pieces have been performed once already (by Webern in 1921 in Berlin at the Austrian Music Festival), we will only be able to refer to the planned new performance as a "first complete performance". But I will be delighted to take this opportunity—should the pieces really find a place in your next season's programme—to start work on the retouching which I have been planning to undertake for so long. . . . And—this I can promise you right now—I shall come for the last rehearsals of these pieces; they are still—after being considered problematic for almost fifteen years without being it at all—a matter of the utmost importance to me!'

Four weeks before the Oldenburg performance of the Orchestral Pieces Schüler asked Berg for an article about his work for the printed programme of the concert. Berg was on the point of leaving for the Düsseldorf première of *Wozzeck* and lacked the time to write the article. But on 2nd April 1930 he sent Schüler some 'quickly marshalled analytical remarks' about the pieces, and these were worked into the following brief analysis by Dr Fritz Uhlenbruch, editor of the programme book:

It is interesting to observe how a symphonic process is concentrated into the three pieces 'Präludium', 'Reigen' and 'Marsch'; that is, how an approximation of the form of a four-movement symphony is achieved in the design. The Präludium would represent the first movement; 'Reigen' contains scherzo and slow movement (in that order!), and the March could be considered the last movement of the 'supposed' symphony. This 'supposition' rests on the constructional working of the pieces (for example the long, development-type passages in the third piece), and it is intended to point out the exceptionally clear and confident architecture of Berg's works.

In considering the individual pieces one recognizes in each one a certain binarity and symmetry. In the first piece several groups of bars in the first and second parts correspond to each other as mirror images, as for example the first and last bars of the percussion. In 'Reigen' the binarity is given by the sequence of scherzo and slow movement mentioned above; this is marked purely externally by the changeover from waltz time to common time (4/2 and 4/4). In the third piece the binarity results from the juxtaposition of the 'march-like' group and the actual 'march' itself (from bar 53 onwards). The 'development' of all the preceding material follows in bar 130, and this is at the same time the coda of the piece.

Alban Berg to the Frankfurt Opera House
Composed summer 1930 for the Fiftieth Jubilee of the Opera House

This canon, based on a twelve-tone theme from Schönberg's opera *Von heute auf morgen*, serves as a souvenir of the first performance of the work in Frankfurt on 1st February 1930

WOZZECK

The following remarks are for the most part my adaptation—undertaken in 1930 under Berg's supervision—of his introductory lecture written in 1929 (see pp. 77–78). (It should be mentioned that Berg originally gave the opera the opus number 7. Later he abandoned opus numbers for this and all succeeding works. His jocular reason for this was that he was ashamed of having produced so few works in such a long period of time.)

Looking back over Berg's stylistic development from the *Early Songs* to *Wozzeck* it is easy to see it as an unbroken increase in his spiritual and sensual powers of design, in the course of which the atonal method of composition conquers the large, far-flung forms. But we must not overlook the radical difference that separates the big and little monologues of the preceding works from the totality of *Wozzeck* as a dramatic whole. The division between the process of maturation and the mastery that is finally attained has seldom been so sharply delineated as in the case of Berg. Patiently he applied himself to all the different departments of his craft before deciding, at the age of thirty-six, to undertake the composition of his first opera.

The decision was triggered by that theatrical performance in the spring of 1914. It is hardly possible to construct a continuous rational motivational connection through from this starting point to the final form of the work. For in the opera the action takes place on two levels simultaneously: in the foreground the realistic drama of poor people, which is unfailingly effective even in the speaking theatre when tautly directed; and in the background the action on mythical levels, which only comes out in the music. The music follows the man Wozzeck into the abyss which he sees opening before him. The relationship, often emphasized by Berg himself, with psychoanalysis, the function of the music as representation and illumination of the unconscious is not to be understood as an analogical translation of the analytical method into musical terms. This function of the music has its origin in Berg's attitude to form, in his firm decision to find out the hidden drives that lie behind the directly visible scenic events, and interpret them in musical symbols. The tragedy of the poor soldier Wozzeck, persecuted and mutilated by the sentimental stupidity and spurious cleverness of his superiors, betrayed by his lover; how he becomes a murderer, and avenges himself on the rest and on himself—this is not an opera on the actions of states, nor yet a social opera; it is naked inwardness, made transparent by the interpretative power of the music.

Berg's eminent musico-dramatic gifts will be apparent even to someone who has not heard a note of the *Wozzeck* music, if he compares Berg's arrangement of the text with the versions contained in the various editions of Büchner's work. Rudolf Schäfke points out (in an article in 'Melos', Berlin, May 1926) various refinements of Berg's textual arrangement, and errs only insofar as he assumes that Berg used Paul Landau's critically sifted edition of 1909, whereas in fact the composer worked from Karl Emil Franzos' first edition of 1879 and only compared his version with other editions after the opera was completed.

Berg's main achievement in the arrangement of the text, apart from linguistic changes of great impact, lies in the logical ordering and tightening up of the action, sketched by Büchner only in a fragmentary manner. By omission[1] and contraction Berg succeeded in reducing the twenty-six scenes of the original to fifteen, the sequence of which, distributed over three acts, is reminiscent of the traditional dramatic scheme of exposition, peripetia and catastrophe.

By his manner of arranging the text, Berg had now achieved dramatic consistency; now—much more difficult—he had to set about forging a musical unity and consistency, without recourse to the means that had been most efficacious in achieving this in the past, namely the manufacture of harmonic relations of tonality. There is a reason deep in Berg's nature why he could not simply override the traditional harmonic principles of dramatic music-making, but had to strive with all his power to preserve a relationship with these principles despite his 'atonality'.

In the places where in a tonal work of art the clear return and establishment of the main key is apparent even to the lay-man, there in *Wozzeck* too the harmonic circle of the large formal sections should close. This consolidation is achieved in the first place by the fact that each act moves towards one and the same final chord, as if forming a cadence, and rests there as if on a tonic chord. These final chords appear each time in a different guise, although they consist of the same notes, for Berg's will to musical consistency and relatedness is comple-mented by his unremitting striving for the largest possible variety in the musical shapes.

From the purely musical construction of each of the three acts we can infer that in *Wozzeck* we are dealing by and large with the well-tried ternary form A–B–A. We can infer this from a certain architectonic parallelism between the first and third acts. These two acts flank the considerably longer and weightier central act in a sort of temporal symmetry. And whereas the form of the central act is a closed, symphonic shape, the form of the outside acts is much looser. Each consists of five loosely related pieces of music corresponding to the loosely strung together scenes. One can describe the five scenes of the first act as 'character pieces', each one characterizing a new main figure in the drama, naturally always in his relationship to the title hero. The five scenes of the third act retain their con-sistency by the application of certain unifying principles which justify the appellation 'inventions' for the musical forms. These forms are linked with the situations rather than with the persons.

In his efforts to achieve musical variety without 'composing through' each of the many scenes in the manner of a Wagnerian music-drama,[2] there was virtually no alternative but to give each scene a different shape, which would acquire consistency from the unity of the musical form. The application of these to the drama resulted just as naturally as the selection of the forms introduced for this purpose. And these forms produced the musical relatedness of the details.

So the application of 'old forms' which caused so much discussion as soon as the opera appeared did not spring at all from any tendency towards archaism, and it would be still more misguided to suppose that the use of such forms had anything to do with the atavistic movement 'Back to . . .' (a movement that started much later anyway). And in fact Berg did not content himself with the 'old forms' alone, he struck out boldly and used other forms based on completely new principles.

Another reason why Berg had to proceed with as much variety and as wide a range of musical shapes as possible was the large number of transitional passages necessitated by the triple change of scene in each act. Here too Berg achieved a diversity rich in contrasts: he designed the transitional passages sometimes as symphonic interludes, and sometimes in the form of a coda to the preceding scene or an introduction to the following one, or both simultaneously. He either endeavoured to connect the discrepant parts of the individual musical forms as unobtrusively as possible, or he preferred to accentuate the contrasts as sharply as he could, throwing them into relief with naked juxtapositions.

The table opposite, suggested by Berg himself, throws light on the sequence of the most important scenic and musical events.

The subsequent remarks on the individual scenes must be limited to brief indications intended to clarify particular methods of procedure or more profound relationships. But to give some slight idea of the unbelievable richness in reference of this dramatic music-making let us try, at least for the first scene of the opera, to demonstrate the thematic construction.[3]

SCENE		MUSIC

ACT I

Wozzeck in his relation to the world around him		*Five character pieces*
Wozzeck and the Captain	scene 1	Suite
Wozzeck and Andres	scene 2	Rhapsody
Marie and Wozzeck	scene 3	Military march and lullaby
Wozzeck and the Doctor	scene 4	Passacaglia
Marie and the Drum Major	scene 5	Andante affettuoso (quasi Rondo)

ACT II

Dramatic development		*Symphony in five movements*
Marie and her child, later Wozzeck	scene 1	Sonata movement
The Captain and the Doctor, later Wozzeck	scene 2	Fantasia and fugue
Marie and Wozzeck	scene 3	Largo
Garden of a public house	scene 4	Scherzo
Guard room in the barracks	scene 5	Rondo con introduzione

ACT III

Catastrophe and epilogue		*Six Inventions*
Marie with the child	scene 1	Invention on a theme
Marie and Wozzeck	scene 2	Invention on a note
Bar	scene 3	Invention on a rhythm
Death of Wozzeck	scene 4	Invention on a hexachord
	(orchestral interlude)	Invention on a tonality
Children playing	scene 5	Invention on a regular quaver movement

That the very first scene of the opera is played in the frame-work of a Suite may be attributed to the fact that the dialogue of this scene, in which nothing really happens, consists merely of various loosely juxtaposed conversational topics. It was necessary to find a small-scale form for each of these topics, so that the whole became a series of little pieces of music, i.e. a Suite. Although it happened unconsciously it was no mere chance that it was a Suite consisting of old forms (though these are stylized to a greater or lesser degree). Musically too this gives the first scene its fitting historical colouring.

The following analysis will show how exactly the selection of the small forms is adapted to the scenic events, making it possible to bind the whole together into a musico-dramatic unity. The strictest regularity pervades even the purely musical aspects; and this is not limited to the most striking thematic events. Each new tempo can be derived almost mathematically from the preceding, as is proved by the metronome figures.[4] The individual short movements are distinguished from one another in the instrumentation; each one has a certain group of instruments as an obligato, and the composition of these different intrumental groups is placed in relation to the action on the stage. Formally, ternary forms predominate (Präludium, Pavane, Gigue and Air), but the reprises are never mere repetitions, rather extensive variations. The Gavotte and the two Doubles are binary, and the cadenzas are free.

ACT I

The first movement of the Suite is a Präludium, with an obligato consisting of five solo woodwinds. It is introduced by two short string chords, joined by a soft side drum roll in crescendo.[5] The first three bars are used later in this scene like a refrain. The Captain's theme appears in bars 4 and 5, and its motivic components provide material for the further construction.

The semiquaver and demi-semiquaver movement in the woodwinds that runs through the whole Präludium corresponds to the Captain's chatty nature, which is crassly apparent in his first words. The middle section (bar 15 with upbeat) consists of an expressive base theme ornamented with arpeggio figures, and at bar 24 this leads back to the reprise. Here we hear Wozzeck's first answer (bars 25–26), his stereotyped 'Jawohl, Herr Hauptmann'; a characteristic motif that gets particular significance in the sequel.

The last notes of the Präludium are led over into the triplet rhythm of the following Pavane in a very artful manner (example 1). Notice the resolution of the syncopations in the

interplay of the two notes D-flat and E-flat, and also the inclusion of the rhythm of bars 25–26!

The Pavane is well suited to the Captain's bombastic images and melancholy observations, and a suitably bombastic instrumental group (percussion) accompanies it. The main theme, which lies in the vocal line, is merely a transformation of the 'refrain', which is taken up again in the Captain's final words 'oder ich werde melancholisch' ('or I'll get melancholy') (bars 47–49).

The Captain's complacent meditation on the subject of the 'Good Man' is aptly clothed in the form of an enthusing viola cadenza. The vocal phrase 'tut alles langsam' ('do everything slowly') (bars 57–58) is imitated successively by horns and double basses.

A Gigue (bar 65) forms the basis for the derisive mocking of Wozzeck. Obligato: four flutes and cello; theme in the cello (bars 67–69). Against this theme, three-part flute runs depict in an intentionally primitive manner 'Schlimm Wetter und Wind' ('Bad weather and wind'). The triplet semiquavers of these passages acquire structural power for the further develop-ment, and reappear in bars 83–89 in held woodwind chords, and from bar 90 in muted brass to illustrate the Captain's silly laughter. His further quips form variations on the Gigue theme: flute, bars 80–83; voice, bars 83–87 and 97–99. A middle section is dominated by the horn theme, bars 73–75 and 76–79 by the rhythmic motif from bars 25–26. Wozzeck has nothing to answer to all this teasing except his stereotyped 'Jawohl, Herr Hauptmann' (bars 25–26), which finally be-comes a droning pedal point. Then at bar 99 the Gigue theme reappears in its original form and leads to a little coda. After this we hear a second cadenza as accompaniment to a new moralistic pose of the Captain's. This second cadenza is a shortened variant[6] of the first one, adapted to the awkward character of the double bassoon, and it forms the bridge into the real moral sermon, which proceeds as a grave Gavotte with an obligato of four trumpets.

The Gavotte opens in the voice part in bar 114 'like a fan-fare'; this is immediately imitated by the trumpets. The refer-ence to the words of the garrison chaplain (bar 120) is echoed by the orchestra in bars 125–126 ('like the full organ'). The first Double contains Wozzeck's rejoinder (the much milder-sounding horns; the melody placed low), and the second Double is the Captain's furious reply (muted trombones fortissimo!). Thematically both Doubles are repetitions of the Gavotte, intensified rhythmically and metrically. But despite strict analogy in the sequence of themes, the variants get pro-gressively more concentrated. The proportions of the numbers of bars are 12 : 6 : 3.

Wozzeck's tormented outburst (bar 136) over the pedal point from bars 25–26 presents the most important motif of the opera. The text itself 'Wir arme Leut' ('We poor people') summarizes the whole social milieu of the work. Musically, this lyrical climax is couched in the form of a ternary Air, with the sound of the strings predominating. The theme of bar 120 reappears in the middle section (bars 139–140), and is fol-lowed in bar 145 by the canon for solo strings (bar 136). Later the motif of bars 25–26 is prominent as the bass of a mighty build-up (bars 149–153) which breaks off suddenly (bar 153) and leaves the two chords of the first bar like an echo, broken up into semiquavers, played by the five solo woodwinds.

The Captain's soothing words lead into the reprise of the Präludium which is inverted crabwise to correspond to the

conversation, which runs backwards. Bars 157–169 correspond
to bars 14–16 of the opening.

The transitional music works over the most important themes
of the Suite like a development section: from bar 173 the Pavane
theme appears in canon in the trumpets, horns and trombones,
and the harp plays the original triplet accompaniment. From
bar 177 we hear the Gavotte motif of bar 125 in canon between
woodwinds, violas and cellos. At bar 180 the three chord
motif from the Gigue (bars 86–88) enters with the beginning
of the Gavotte (bar 114), and at bar 181 the horn passage from
bar 73 joins in and also the Gigue theme (bar 80), and the
bass of bars 180–192 corresponds to bars 114–119. The change
of time at bar 183 brings in the three-part flute runs accompanying the Gigue, this time in violins and violas, together with
the middle section of the Air (bars 183–192 correspond to bars
139–142) and the Gavotte theme from bar 114. At bar 191 the
violins enter 'drowning everything' with bar 136 and its
natural continuation (137–138). In the bass we hear bars 25–26
and in the woodwinds bar 142. The final build-up of the Air
is then brought in, similarly varied: the violins in bars 195–200
correspond to the voice in bars 151–153; parts of the cadenza
of bars 55–57 are woven into this, played this time by the
cello (bars 195–200); a variation of bar 136 is introduced in bars
198–200 in canon in trumpets, horns and pizzicato strings.

The last chord is quickly damped and sounds on softly into
the beginning of the next scene, the atmosphere of which is
in complete contrast to that of the preceding. The narrow,
musty barrack room is superseded by the 'open field', a stage
above and below which the elemental forces have free play, no
longer separated by any wall from the man they are to claim
as their own. The musical form of this scene is described by
Berg as a 'Rhapsody'. However malleable to the requirements
of the scenic action, and despite the freedom of the thematic
working, this musical formation has nothing in common with
the earlier improvisatory, potpourri-type Rhapsodies; it obeys
strict rules. The elements of the musical action are: A, the

series of chords I II III; B, the hunting song; and C, the chromatic four‑note motif (example 2). The beginning of the

Rhapsody (bars 201–209) is dominated by A and C, which can be regarded as quasi 'Nature' sounds. (Incidentally the three chords of A appear also in Act II in the snores of the sleeping soldiers, and there too they are a 'Nature' sound of humanity vegetating in the guard room.) In the whole scene C plays the part of a general 'bridge motif'; to start with it leads to the first entry of the hunting song (bars 210–211).[7] Schäfke, in his article, represents the formal construction of the whole scene in the following way:

201–222	223–245	245–268	269–298	299–329	
Wozzeck and Andres	Wozzeck	Andres	Wozzeck	Wozzeck and Andres	
Exposition of A and B	First develop‑ ment of A	Develop‑ ment of B	Second devel‑ opment of A	Coda: and reference to B	
C	C	C	C	C	C

In its repeated appearances A is progressively richer in instru‑ mentation and melodically extended; B is elaborated in the voice part in the first repetition, and in the orchestra in the second repetition. Wozzeck's words 'Es wandert was mit uns da unten!' ('Something is moving with us down there!') (bars 273–278) are backed by a motif from the March in the Three Orchestral Pieces (bars 79–83). The build‑up that develops over the 'step motif' of a descending major second is followed

by a long held wind chord, damped suddenly 'quasi harmonics'. Musically, this sharply accentuates the contrast in this scene
between Wozzeck's exalted behaviour and lifeless Nature,
which inspires him with fear. C in the form of a chromatic
scale on the timpani provides the transition to the Coda,
which is based on A but with the three chords in the order
III II I. With a walking descending scale of crotchets A becomes a closing song in which we hear 'as if in the distance' the
Austrian military calls 'zum Gebet' (bar 312 in the horn) and
'Abgeblasen' (bar 317, clarinet), as well as fragments of B.
C, gradually reverberating away in the basses, forms the
orchestral background for the approaching military March of
the stage music, which dominates the beginning of the third
scene.

The same applies to the popular elements in the March and
Marie's Lullaby as to the hunting song in the preceding scene.
At the beginning of the Trio (bar 349) the March melody
divides into two opposing voices. These are only reunited in
bar 354 with the re-entry of the main section. The repetition of
the March becomes suddenly inaudible (bar 363) when the
window is slammed shut. The delicate colours of the string
writing (solo strings *divisi*) form an effective contrast to the
noisy wind music. Marie's outburst 'Komm, mein Bub!'
('Come, my boy') presents us with a theme (example 3) that is

important in the sequel as a 'plaint motif' and provides the
transition to the lullaby. The characteristic steps of a fourth in
the Lullaby have already been anticipated not only melodically
and rhythmically by timpani and harp, but also harmonically,
by the 6/4 chords that preponderate throughout this passage.
The instrumental ending of the song gives way to a cadential
passage of open fifths. These fifths reappear several times in the

course of the opera, and seem to represent Marie's attitude of
waiting for something unknown. Bars 415–426 contain a little
ternary form devoted to Marie deep in her thoughts. Bars 415–
416 correspond to bars 425–426; this is one of the few points
of rest in the opera. The soft fragments of the military March in
the middle section betray the real object of Marie's musings. The
repetition of the motif of fifths is interrupted by the hasty,
impetuous motif (example 4) (bar 427) of Wozzeck suddenly

knocking at the window. From this point on the musical construction of this scene abandons any formal scheme and proceeds in a manner reminiscent of the style of Wagner and his
age, who liked to 'compose through' long stretches of text in
this way, using only the *leit-motivs* as supports. But in this case
each idea is derived from the preceding in a logical stream, and
the 'leit-motivs', besides their absolute musical symbolic force,
have only to fulfil their function as 'guarantees', which we
mentioned earlier in this book. In any case, this is the only place
in the whole opera where Berg dispensed with any kind of
formal control. When Wozzeck speaks of his visions we hear
appropriate quotations from the preceding scene (but with a
totally different instrumental colouring): bars 435–437 correspond to bars 290–293, bars 443–446 to bars 239–243. The
second quotation with the text from the Bible crops up frequently when Wozzeck's dim religiosity—losing itself in
mystical spheres—seeks to express itself. At the words 'Es ist
hinter mir hergegangen' ('It followed behind me') the basses
sound the 'walking motif' from bar 271, while the voice
takes up the horn theme (273 ff.) from the Orchestral Pieces.
There follows an analogous build-up to the climax when
Wozzeck cries 'Was soll das werden?' ('What is supposed to
become of it?') (bar 449 corresponds to bar 270). It is highly
remarkable how Berg achieves the same musico-dramatic

20, 21   A postcard sent to Erich Kleiber on 27th November 1934, referring to the soprano part in the Lulu Symphony.   The other side shows a picture of the Opera House, Unter den Linden, where, on 30th November 1934, the première of the Lulu Symphony took place

22 Manon Gropius, to whose memory Berg dedicated his Violin Concerto

effect while completely changing the instrumentation. Wozzeck's hasty exit is again accompanied by the hasty motif
in analogy to his entry; here it appears in inversion. Previously
we have heard the chords III II I, joined by a whole tone scale
in the top part, as an ending to the bitonal effects that are frequently prominent in this scene. Marie is left behind with her
confusion and her child; the suffering of her soul is accompanied
by the motif of seconds (bar 462) in muted horns. The motif
in the double basses in bar 461 is derived from her words
'Er schnappt noch über . . .' ('He will go crazy . . .'). The transitional music, which reaches its climax in bar 476, is a short
development of the most important themes of this scene and the
preceding one; to end, it lands on the harmony A, D-sharp,
B, F (bar 484). Now a solo viola unfolds the harmony notes
E-flat, B and F over a pedal point on A. In bar 486 this is
taken over both melodically and rhythmically by the solo
clarinet.[8] This clarinet passage is a note-for-note, rhythmically
abbreviated anticipation of the Passacaglia theme that forms
the basis of the next scene. This theme is a succession of twelve
different notes which recur in every variation.

The theme is stated in bars 488–495 with the first words of
the scene. It merges completely with the Doctor's speech, and
is almost hidden in the mobile rubato of a cello recitative.
Twenty-one variations follow; called variations with good
reason, for the subject is one and the same theme plus the
Doctor's obsessive *idées fixes*.[9] Even where Wozzeck—tormented by the Doctor and his fixed ideas—takes part in the
conversation we find reverberations of these ideas. It would
require a separate text to analyze all the links in this chain of
variations and point out their wonderful co-ordination with the
individual parts of the text. Here we can only afford a few
short hints as to the general structure and the most important
counterpoints. By and large we can distinguish three main
sections: a first group is made up of the first twelve variations,
which accompany the Doctor's propositions and Wozzeck's
objections. The theme, which is present note for note through-

out the scene, loses itself in the increasing richness of counter⁄
point. A new and more animated cycle begins with the thir⁄
teenth variation; and the topic of conversation has changed too.
Now the Doctor not only wants to use Wozzeck as a guinea⁄
pig in his feeding experiments, he also wants to exploit him
as a psychological curiosity. At the nineteenth variation the
stretto begins; here the Doctor's scientific conceit reaches its
climax. Finally, in the last variation, the Doctor bursts forth
with a cry for immortality, the most ambitious of his fixed ideas.
The theme rises with exaggerated dignity, harmonized like a
choral and played by the full orchestra. At bar 462 it is damped
quickly and returns to the matter⁄of⁄fact dialogue of the scene's
opening.

Here are a few notes on some details of the design of this
scene, which is musically one of the most complicated in the
opera. The Doctor's first words (example 5) (bar 485) run

through the whole scene like a refrain and become an important
link—especially the first phrase (a)—between the individual
variations. Notice too the extraordinary way the Doctor always
declaims the word 'Wozzeck' (b). At bar 491 we hear example
6 in the voice part; this occurs frequently in the sequel as a

characterization of the Doctor's scholastic conceit. In the third
variation the new topic of conversation ('Mutton') is intro⁄
duced (bar 510) by a grotesque counter⁄theme in the trombones.

Wozzeck's insistent remonstrations bring back themes from the preceding scene: from bar 538 we hear the motif of fifths, the military March and the hasty motif, which has already ap⁄ peared in the voice part in bar 524. In the sixth and seventh variations the theme is played by solo strings as two⁄part chords, quite in the manner of the later twelve⁄note technique. In the ninth variation bar 552 corresponds to bar 449. The Nature mood of the second variation calls up extensive remi⁄ niscences from the second scene: bars 554–560 correspond to bars 227–231. In the twelfth variation the theme is again clear and prominent, played by the trumpet. The score has an almost geometric regularity at the point where Wozzeck says 'Linienkreise, Figuren!—Wer das lesen könnte!' ('Line⁄circles, figures!—Who could read that!') The thirteenth and fourteenth variations together constitute a sort of ternary form. At bar 562 the violins introduce a motif which is used later in the second theme of the Fugue in the second act. The eighteenth variation is on a larger scale, and develops a series of motifs from preceding variations. Suggested references to the Doctor's first words bring us to the end of this scene, over a timpani roll on D⁄sharp, the first note of the theme.

The last scene (bars 656 ff.) with its 62 bars is by far the shortest scene in this act—and the same proportion is retained in the other acts. Musically, it is devoted entirely to the charac⁄ terization of the Drum Major's brutal boasting and vitality. Even Marie, although the indication 'affettuoso' applies to her, adopts the Drum Major's way of speaking, as though she wished to identify herself with her erotic ideal. Her part contains many phrases that belong to the style of the Drum Major, for example bars 673, 675, 698, etc. And this coincides with the Rondo form, which does justice to the central idea of the whole scene —the idea of seduction. In this free Rondo we can distinguish two main sections (bars 665–683 and 684–709) and the Coda (bars 710–717); these correspond respectively to the prelimi⁄ nary skirmishing, the seduction itself, and the aftermath. The Rondo theme (example 7) is sharply defined in the first and

third sections; in the second section it is pushed rather into the background by the Drum Major's brutal attacking motif (bar 685) and only reappears in the largely contrapuntal de-velopment from bar 693 onwards. As the curtain rises in bar 666 the Rondo theme appears in a form which always recurs in the sequel, with a rhythm borrowed from the military March. The latter itself is heard shortly afterwards (bars 668–670). The E-flat clarinet motif of bars 656–657 is intended to mirror the Drum-Major's complacent nature. The horn passage in bars 658–659 is important in the sequel (Act II, scenes 4 and 5). Marie's pride in her handsome lover (voice part, bar 675) has already been touched on much earlier (piccolo, bar 339). The cadential progression of the bass to F in bars 677–683 (at the end of the first section) is remarkable. Marie's unaccompanied, fanfare-like cry 'Rühr' mich nicht an!' ('Don't you touch me!') figures as a continuation of the trumpet part (bar 698) and reappears in a parallel passage in the text in Act II, bar 395. The Rondo theme entering at the climax (bar 712) is followed (in bars 713–714) by a postscript which draws bar 675 into the theme. This expositional act—which conceals the germs of the whole future development—finishes over the same pedal point of G and D that accompanied the introduction of the Rondo theme (bars 656 ff.).

ACT II
The first scene, which is in Sonata (first movement) form, is introduced by an orchestral prelude which is closely related to the final scene of the preceding act by its harmony of fourths and fifths. The musico-dramatic reason for the choice of Sonata form is provided by the fact that the three characters concerned (Marie, her child and Wozzeck) are each allotted one of the three thematic groups (main, subsidiary and closing groups) of a Sonata form exposition. The main theme consists

of two phrases which make a proper eight-bar musical sentence (bars 7–15). In the repetition the voices move closer and closer together and prepare the way for the dissonances of seconds in the 'transition' ('principle of the smallest transition'). The transition is a little form on its own (bars 29–42), which runs backwards symmetrically from bar 35. The subsidiary group begins in bar 43, and the Coda in bar 55 (compare Marie's song with the one in Act I!). At bar 60 the first reprise begins, which corresponds to the mechanical repetition used in the classical Sonata scheme. This reprise, though varied and con-tracted, clearly repeats the exposition—a procedure conditioned by the events on stage, which represent a return of the same dramatic situations (Marie looks at her jewellery in the mirror and afterwards wants to put the child to sleep). The develop-ment begins (bar 96) when Wozzeck enters; now the main characters (both human and musical) get to grips with each other. At the climax (bar 114) the motto of 'We poor people' is introduced, drowning everything else. Wozzeck's following words 'Da ist wieder Geld, Marie, die Löhnung . . .' ('Here's some more money, Marie, my pay . . .') are sung against a sustained C major triad in the orchestra, and the diminishing intervals of the hasty counting of the money are imposed on this triad. Berg once said of this passage: 'What clearer expres-sion could be found to express the prosaic quality of this money that they are talking about!' Marie remains alone. The reprise of the Sonata movement begins in bar 128 and, in keeping with the collapse of the opening's bright and friendly mood, it is much lower and gloomier in colour. The transi-tional music (bars 140–170), which forms part of the reprise, is also a unit in itself marked out by a harp glissando which descends *ff* at the beginning and rises *pp* at the end, establishing the relationship with the succeeding scene.

In the second scene there are again three characters on the stage, though they are more loosely related than the near rela-tions who take part in the preceding scene. In the last scene it was possible to find a musical form in which the members

grew together organically like a family (Sonata form); cor׳
respondingly in this scene it was fitting to take a form whose
elements were rather disparate and contrasted. The form of this
scene is a Fantasia and Fugue with three themes; the themes—
in contrast to the themes of a Sonata movement which can run
into one another melodically—appear sharply distinguished
from one another motivically. The themes of the Captain and
the Doctor are familiar from Act I (bars 2 and 562 in Act I),
and Wozzeck's theme, although not stated literally, is clearly
presaged in the preceding Sonata movement. The Fantasia is
ternary (A1 B A2); and B itself is again ternary (a1 b a2).[10]
Numerous correspondences in the details can be found in this
formal scheme, which fits the conversational exchanges ex׳
actly. For example the delegation of the formal sections to the
various participants in the conversation: in A1 the captain
jokes with the Doctor; in B the Doctor frightens the Captain
with his gloomy prognoses; in A2 they both detain Wozzeck
and combine (in the Fugue) in taunting him. A sharp note of
parody is maintained throughout this scene, sometimes rising
to passages that are directly funny, for example the sentimental
harmonization of the Captain's theme in bars 265–266 where
the additional *stretto* in diminution is supposed to represent 'the
pettiness of this pain' (Berg's words), or the passage where the
Captain has a fit of coughing in time to a funeral march
(bars 258–259). The fact that the first two themes both begin
with the interval of a major second is frequently exploited in
the working of these themes. The third theme is introduced
(bars 273–274) by the trombones in three parts (the fourth
trombone maintains the pedal point on E together with the
timpani). In the Fugue each of the three trombone parts (from
bar 313) appears as an independent thematic shape; the first
two themes have previously been developed singly and in
combination. Bars 326–329 constitute a more homophonic
episode which breaks off abruptly with the renewed entry of
the third theme in the second half of bar 329. Now all three
themes are worked over together, the first two themes also

appearing in their inverted forms. Trailing clarinet figures are derived from their basic shapes and these appear to stand literally still 'quite without expression' in bars 366–368.

A Largo, intoned by a special 'chamber orchestra', rises over this foundation. It represents the slow movement of this symphonic act, and at the same time forms the centre piece of the entire opera. The orchestra corresponds exactly to that used by Arnold Schönberg in his Chamber Symphony; Berg wished to express a tribute to his master and friend right in this central position in his work. The Largo is clearly ternary: A1=bars 367–387, B=bars 387–397, A2=bars 397–411. The main theme, played by the solo cello in bars 367–371, is in two sections. The sequel is full of reminiscences of Wozzeck's themes and those of Marie and the Drum Major. In the central section the winds of the chamber orchestra throw in their inter- jections 'quasi molto agitato' without reference to the conduct of the main orchestra. We have already mentioned the parallel with Act I, bar 698 where Marie says 'Rühr' mich nicht an!' ('Don't you touch me!'). The whole Largo, especially bar 398 with the words 'Lieber ein Messer . . .' ('Rather a knife . . .') is closely connected with the murder scene in Act III; it ends over a pedal point on F-sharp, the dominant of the fateful B which dominates the later scene. The Largo comes to rest on the same harmony, which, set in motion once more, forms the same clarinet figurations (in reverse) that provided the chord in bar 368. These figurations also lead into the transitional music, which introduces the next scene with a slow Ländler.

The next scene constitutes the Scherzo of the dramatic sym- phony of this act. The Ländler (412–447)[11] is the first idea of this Scherzo; the journeymen's song (bars 447–480) makes a first Trio; the Waltz music on stage (bars 481–559) is the second Scherzo; and the journeymen's hunting chorus (bars 560–589)—the centre piece of the whole—constitutes a second Trio. Now there follows—in keeping with the strict construc- tion of such Scherzo movements (think for example of the Scherzos in Schumann's symphonies)—a repetition of the first three-part Scherzo group. This repetition is not literal, but varied to the utmost according to the progress of the action. The Ländler is quoted exactly in the stage music (bars 590–604), but placed in completely new musical surroundings. The first Trio—represented by the journeymen's song—is repeated in bars 615–650, but in a form so changed that the basic harmonies (bars 456 ff.) are taken apart to provide a Chorale melody in minims. Further: in bars 604–635 this is given to the bombardon and provides the basis for the whole melo-dramatic parody of a sermon. (So this melodrama is on the one hand the repeat of the first Trio, and on the other a proper, though parodistic, five-part Chorale!) Besides this, the har-monies of bars 456 ff. have already been anticipated in bars 447–449 in the form of pure movement. Example 8 shows these harmonies in the three different guises in which they

appear. The brief entry of the hunting chorus (bars 636–639) is a reference to the second Trio. The Fool's scene (bars 643–670) is the bridge leading to the repetition of the first Scherzo; bars 640–649 are a reprise in reverse of bars 447–455 (though the colouring is completely changed). The repetition of the stage musician's Waltz preserves the character of the Waltz, but —since it forms the transitional music to the next scene—it is executed in the expanded form of a symphonic development in the full orchestra.[12]

When the transitional music suddenly breaks off we hear, the curtain still closed, the snoring chorus (intended as a 'Nature sound') of the soldiers in the guard room. Wozzeck's visions (bars 744–758) are accompanied by reminiscences of the Ländler scene and the 'open field'. The Rondo Martiale which begins in bar 761 is scenically and musically the parallel of the corresponding scene in Act I. (Musically, the fight be-tween Wozzeck and the Drum Major is no different from that between Marie and the Drum Major in the parallel scene. The outcome in both cases is a heavy defeat for Wozzeck.) But whereas the Rondo form is only hinted at in the passionate Andante of Act I, here we have to deal with a Rondo con-structed strictly according to the rules (in accord with the almost military ruling of the fight). The theme (bars 761–764) is introduced three more times (bars 774, 785, and 805). Two subsidiary passages are inserted, the first beginning at bar 768 and the second at the upbeat to bar 776. The second is also developed in inversion (bar 779) and later canonically (bar 800). Further, the theme of the 'poor people' and the military March are also introduced. The Rondo ends with the chord common to the endings of all three acts; this time it is resolved gradually into its component parts, these being reduced from six voices to one voice, finally leaving only the low B as a last remainder—the note which governs the musical action of the murder scene. Here, where the decision to kill has been finalized, it is played by the harp *pppp*, underlined by a soft stroke on the tam-tam.

ACT III

Berg himself frequently emphasized the strict architectonic structure of the first scene, which represents an 'invention on a theme'. Schäfke's article deals with this scene in detail and was fully approved by Berg, so we restrict ourselves here to a few supplementary remarks. The number 7 plays a large part in the

Passage from *Wozzeck*, Act III

construction: the 7-bar theme consists of a statement and answer that express straight away the contrast in mood between the objective Bible text read aloud by Marie, and her own painful subjective reflections on it. This contrast runs through the whole scene. The two halves of the theme are joined by a double chord which combines the tonic and the Neapolitan sixth; this chord is important in the sequel. The theme is varied seven times, each variant being seven bars long, and the closing double fugue has—in accord with the duality of the theme—two seven-note subjects and 3×7 bars. The passage pertaining to the child (bars 19–21) is dominated by the theme devoted to him in the first scene of Act II. Marie's telling of the fairy tale (fifth variation and first two bars of the sixth) is intentionally tonal (F minor); the tonality is supposed to symbolize, like a quotation, the vanished world of the fairy tale.

The Fugue, which is at the same time the bridge to the next scene, ends with the double chord mentioned above, with the double basses playing the low B 'foreign to the harmony' which governs form and context in the music of the second scene. It appears in the most manifold ways imaginable: as a pedal point, as a stationary middle or top part, in octaves, and in all conceivable registers and timbres. Apart from this, the music of this scene is rich in reminiscences of preceding material; the Largo in Act II in particular is frequently quoted. When finally—with timpani strokes on B growing to the most extreme *ff*—Marie is murdered, we hear, over the pedal point, a tumultuous sequence of all the musical figures associated with her. As may be the case in the moment of death, the most important elements in life pass by the dying person in distorted form and like lightning: the Lullaby, the jewellery scene from Act II, the Drum Major's theme, Wozzeck's hastiness, the Plaint motif, and finally, at her last breath, dissolving into the motif of open fifths—the theme of her futile waiting.

The short piece of transitional music that follows is still occupied with the stationary B, this time as a unison—almost the only note in the whole scale which can be played by almost all the instruments of the large orchestra (example 9). The crescendo grows from the softest possible entry of the muted

horn through the successive and ever more powerful entries of the whole orchestra (without percussion). It is an irresistible effect, and in every performance of *Wozzeck* it literally drags the audience from their seats. As the music example shows, the entries do not occur at regular intervals, but obey a peculiar rhythmic law; the wind entries and the string entries each produce a particular rhythm, and the two groups of entries interact canonically at the interval of a crotchet. The apparent irregularity produced in this way—the listener is naturally no more aware of this than he is of the logical order of the entries —breathes a particularly vital force into the crescendo note, for it becomes clear that this crescendo has a much greater dynamic effect than it does in the repetition, where the B appears in all the different registers and is further supported by the whole percussion section.

The rhythm of Example 9 is of course not a chance product, any more than the chord (bar 114) (example 10) to which the

unison crescendo leads. Both have important thematic signifi-cance. The rhythm is the basis of the entire third scene and— demonstrable in every bar—guarantees its unity. But it does not

force itself on the music of this scene in the manner of a contin﹣
uous ostinato; it is introduced in such a way as to permit of ex﹣
treme metrical variety within this quasi﹣rhythmical uniformity.
Either melodies are set on this rhythm, as for example the wild,
fast Polka played by the stage piano at the beginning of the
scene, or it serves as a basis for the instrumental accompani﹣
ment; in either case it may appear in diminution, augmentation,
triplets, *stretto*, shifted, etc., in the further course of the scene.
The motivic work contains reminiscences of Marie's death
(bar 152 ff. in the horns), and of the Waltz development in
Act II (bar 180 ff.=Act II bar 670 ff.). Wozzeck's song
(bar 144 ff.) corresponds melodically with the Lullaby.

The last canonic climax of the main rhythm in the tran﹣
sitional music leads to the hexachord B C F A D E, which
sounds in the beginning of the next scene like an echo, and
finds there (bar 220) its harmonic completion in B﹣flat C﹣
sharp E G﹣sharp E﹣flat F. Both of these hexachords have been
prepared in the culminating chord (example 10) of the great
unison crescendo. The manner of exploiting musical material
that proved its worth earlier in the matter of a note and a rhythm
is now applied to the second of the hexachords, which provides
the design principle for the fourth scene. Despite the subordina﹣
tion of this scene to the hexachord, here too the greatest variety
and colourfulness has been obtained by submitting the hexa﹣
chord—just as was the case with the single note and the rhythm
—to all imaginable variations, as for instance: subdivision,
transformation into a melodic line, inversion, variations of
register and timbre. Architectonically, a symmetrical ternary
form is obtained by using the hexachord only on one step of
the scale (naturally with all its variants) in the outside sections,
while in the middle section it visits all the steps of the chromatic
scale. When finally the hexachord returns to its original position
(bar 315)—one can even say its tonal centre—it forms the
harmonic bridge to the following orchestral interlude, whose
key of D minor is just the chromatic resolution of the hexa﹣
chord.[13]

The interlude should be understood within the musico-dramatic architecture of the opera as an 'epilogue' following Wozzeck's suicide; it is a personal statement of the author, who steps back, away from the theatrical events (compare Büchner's epilogue 'The poet speaks . . .'). Musically this last interlude represents a development—analogous to the mourning music in *Götterdämmerung*—of all the more important thematic figures that have had a bearing on Wozzeck in the course of the opera. They are all held together by the unifying principle of tonality.[14] The tonality of D minor is stretched to its extreme limits in the course of this ternary piece. The opening with the hexachord has already been mentioned; in the middle section the thematic work thickens into a sort of developmental *stretto* leading to a climax in bar 364 on a chord that—although it includes all twelve notes of the chromatic scale—sounds, in the framework of this tonality, as a clear dominant harmony which leads back quite naturally to the D minor of the reprise. The following 3/4 bars gradually prepare the way for the 4/4 of bar 371. The synchronized change in this rhythm provides the flowing triplet quavers (notated in 12/8 time) of the final scene.

The unrelenting quaver movement of the children's scene—the melodic line is decisively determined by the Lullaby—represents a 'perpetuum mobile' in the sense of the old text books of form. It is a uniform principle of design that is appropriate not only to the children's game but also to the profoundly melancholy ending of the whole work. Besides the Lullaby, we hear reminiscences of Marie's 'plaint motif' and the motif of her futile waiting. The orchestra is reduced in size in a particular way to create a delicate, child-like sound. Although bars 389–392 are a clear cadential progression towards the final chord, it almost seems as if the music would go on further, as life itself moves on beyond the existence of the individual. In fact, the opening bars of the work could quite easily follow directly after these final bars and close the fateful circle of the opera with sadness and solace combined.

CHAMBER CONCERTO FOR PIANO AND VIOLIN WITH THIRTEEN WIND INSTRUMENTS

The open letter that we reproduce here, in which Berg dedicates his Chamber Concerto to Arnold Schönberg, was first printed in the Viennese musical magazine 'Pult und Taktstock' (February 1925).

9th February 1925

My dear honoured friend Arnold Schönberg!

The composition of this Concerto, dedicated to you on your fiftieth birthday, has been completed only today, on my fortieth birthday. Though late presented, I beg you nonetheless to accept it in a spirit of friendship; all the more so since it has also turned out—though intended for you from the start—to be a little memorial to a friendship now twenty years old. In a musical motto that precedes the first movement the letters of your name, Webern's and my names have been captured—as far as is possible in musical notation[15]—in three themes (or motifs) which have been allotted an important rôle in the melodic development of this music.

This already announces a *trinity of events*, and such a trinity —it is after all a matter of your birthday, and all the good things, that I wish you, makes three—is also important for the whole work:

The three parts of my Concerto, united in a single movement, are characterized by the following three headings or tempo indications:

I Thema scherzoso con Variazioni
II Adagio
III Rondo ritmico con Introduzione (cadenza)

A particular sound body is proper to each of these, whereby I have made use of the trinity of available instrumental families (keyboard, stringed, and wind instruments). First the piano (I), then the violin (II), and finally both of the concertante instru׳ ments are set against the accompanying wind ensemble.

The ensemble itself (which with the violin and the piano makes up a chamber orchestra *fifteen* strong—a holy number for this kind of instrumental combination since your Opus 9) consists of: piccolo, flute, oboe, cor anglais, clarinets in E׳flat and A, bass clarinet, bassoon, double bassoon; two horns, trumpet and trombone.

Formally too the number three or its multiples keeps cropping up:

In the *first* movement we find a six׳fold recurrence of the same basic idea. This idea, stated like an exposition by the wind ensemble as a ternary variations theme of 30 bars, is repeated by the piano alone in the virtuoso character of that instrument, thus constituting a first variant (first reprise). Variation 2 presents the melody notes of the 'theme' in inversion; variation 3 uses them in retrograde order; and variation 4 uses the inversion of the retrograde form (these three middle varia׳ tions can be regarded as a sort of development section in this 'sonata first movement'). The last variation returns to the theme's basic shape. But this occurs in the form of *stretti* be׳ tween piano and wind ensemble (these are canons in which a group of voices that enters later tries to overtake another group that entered first, succeeds in doing this, flies past and leaves the first group far behind), so this last variation (or reprise) also acquires a totally new shape, corresponding to its simul׳ taneous position as coda. It is not really necessary to draw atten׳ tion to this fact, since obviously every one of these transforma׳ tions of the theme has its own profile, although—and it *does* seem important to say this—the scherzo character predominates throughout this first part.

The structure of the *Adagio* is also based on 'ternary song form': A1–B–A2 where A2 is the inversion of A1. The

23   At the Waldhaus, Summer 1935

24   The last photograph of Berg, taken at the end of November 1935

repetition of this first half of the movement (120 bars) takes place in retrograde form, partly a free formation of the reversed thematic material, but partly—as for example the whole of the middle section B—in the form of an exact mirror image.

The *third* movement, finally, is an amalgamation of the two preceding movements (see the tabular general survey!). As a consequence of the repetition of the variation movement that this necessitates—although it is enriched by the simultaneous reprise of the Adagio—the architectonic construction of the whole Concerto also manages to be ternary in form.

The uniting of movements I and II produced three impor/ tant methods of combination:

1. free counterpointing of the parts corresponding to one another;
2. the successive juxtaposition of individual phrases and little sections, like a duet, and
3. the exact summation of whole passages from both move/ ments.

The problem of collecting all these disparate components and characters under one roof (just think, honoured friend: on the one hand a variation movement of circa nine minutes dura/ tion, scherzoso throughout, and on the other a broadly sung, extended Adagio lasting a quarter of an hour!), of making a new movement out of them with a quite independent tone, resulted in the form of the 'Rondo ritmico'.[16]

Three rhythmic forms: a main rhythm, a subsidiary rhythm, and a rhythm that can be considered as a sort of motif, are laid under the melody notes of the main and subsidiary voices. The rhythms occur with manifold variations—extended and abbreviated, augmented and diminished, in *stretto* and in reverse, and in all imaginable metrical shifts and transposi/ tions, etc., etc. Thematic unity is obtained by means of these rhythms and their recurrence according to the design of the Rondo. This unity is nowise inferior to that of the old Rondo form, and guarantees the relatively easy 'intelligibility'—if I may make use of one of your technical terms—of the musical action.

Tabular General Survey

I	Thema	Var. I	II	III	IV	V	Number of bars
Thema con Variazioni	in the basic shape		retrograde	inversion	retrograde inversion	basic shape	
	(Expo- sition)	(First reprise)		(Development)		(Second reprise)	
	bars: 30	30	60	30	30	60	240 ⎤
II Adagio		*Ternary* A1 B	A2	A2	*Retrograde* B	A1	
			(inversion of A1)		(mirror form of preceding B)		480 ⎤
	bars: 30 12 36		12 30	30	12 36	12 30	240 ⎦
							96⟨
III (=I plus II) Rondo ritmico con Introduzione	Introduction (cadenza for violin and piano) bars: 54	Exposition 96	Development (da capo) 79			Second reprise or coda 76	305 ⎤ 480 ⎦ 175 ⎦
		Repeat: 175					

It was in a scene in my opera *Wozzeck* that I showed for the first time the possibility of this method of allotting such an important *constructive* rôle to a rhythm. But that a degree of thematic transformation on the basis of a rhythm such as I have attempted in the Rondo under discussion is admissible, was proved to me by a passage in your Serenade, where in the last movement (admittedly for quite different motives) you place a number of motifs and themes from preceding movements on rhythms that do not belong to them from the start; and vice versa. And I have just read an article by Felix Greissle (Anbruch, February 1925) about the formal foundations of your Wind Quintet in which he writes, among other things, in the last sentence 'The theme always has the same rhythm, but in each case it is made up of notes from a different series', and this seems to me to be further proof of the rightness of such a rhythmic method of construction.

The choice of *time signatures* provided another means of setting the finale of my Concerto on its own feet (despite the fact that all the notes are dependent on those of the first two movements). The whole of the variations movement was in *triple* time; the Adagio is predominantly in *duple* time; the Rondo on the other hand is constantly changing between all conceivable even and odd, simple and compound metres, so that in the metrical field too I accentuated the ever-recurrent trinity of events.

This is also expressed in the *harmony*: besides the long stretches of completely dissolved tonality, there are individual shorter passages with a tonal flavour, and also passages that correspond to the laws set up by you for 'composition with twelve notes related only to one another'. Finally I should mention that the *number of bars*, both in the whole work and in the individual sections, was also determined by divisibility by three; I realize that—insofar as I make this generally known—my reputation as a mathematician will grow in proportion (. . . to the square of the distance) as my reputation as a composer sinks.

But seriously: if in this analysis I have spoken almost exclusively of things connected with the number three, this is because, firstly, it is just those aspects that will be ignored by everybody (in favour of other more musical aspects); secondly, because as an author it is much easier to speak about such external matters than about inward processes, in which respect this Concerto is certainly no poorer than any other music. I can tell you, dearest friend, that if it became known how much friendship, love, and a world of human and spiritual references I have smuggled into these three movements, the adherents of programme music—should there be any left—would go mad with joy; and the representatives and defenders of 'New Classicism', and 'New Matter-of-factness', the 'Linearists' and 'Physiologists', the 'Counterpointists' and 'Formalists' would rush to attack me, outraged by my 'romantic' leanings, if I were to let slip the fact that they too—if they take the trouble to seek out their respective references—are taken into account in the work.

For it was in the intention of this dedication really to bring you 'all good things' on your birthday, and the 'Concerto' is the very art-form in which not only the soloists (including the conductor!) have the chance of show off their brilliance and virtuosity, the author can too, for once. Many years ago, honoured friend, you advised me to write such a work, if possible with chamber orchestral accompaniment; it never crossed your mind then (or perhaps it did?!) that with this piece of advice—as with everything you said and did—you were anticipating a time when just this genre would awake to new life. And, as I hand it to you now to mark a three-fold jubilee as I said at the outset, I can hope to have found one of those 'better occasions' of which you wrote prophetically in your *Harmonielehre*:

'And so this movement too will perhaps return to me once more.'

Your ALBAN BERG

LYRIC SUITE FOR STRING QUARTET

This work was completed in 1926. It had its première in Vienna on 8th January 1927, played by Rudolf Kolisch's 'Neuen Wiener Streichquartett' who performed it thereafter about a hundred times in public. Berg wrote a thematic analysis of the work for Kolisch (who was a good friend of his) and I published this analysis in facsimile in my little book of memoirs (*Alban Berg. Bildnis im Wort, Selbstzeugnisse und Aussagen der Freunde* published by 'Die Arche', Zurich 1959). The most important elements of the analysis are reproduced in the following:

Six movements: Allegretto (12-note)
                Andante (free)
                Allegro (12-note, Trio free)
                Adagio (free)
                Presto (free, the two Trios 12-note)
                Largo (12-note)

The series is changed in the course of the four movements by altering the position of a few notes. (These changes are unimportant as regards the line, but important as regards the characters —'submitting to fate'.)

Connection of the individual movements is performed—apart from the fact that the twelve-note series establishes such a connection—by taking a component (a theme or a series, a passage or an idea) from one movement and entering it in the following movement; the last movement reaches back into the first movement. Naturally not mechanically but in relation to the large evolution (build-up of mood) within the *whole* piece ('submitting to fate'!).

I *Allegretto gioviale* (introductory character, quasi Intrada)
Series of the first movement
=F E C A G D A-flat D-flat E-flat G-flat B-flat B
=the twelve-note series found by F. H. Klein, containing all
twelve intervals in a symmetrical arrangement (the only
one of its kind). Two symmetrical halves at the interval of
a diminished fifth (which plays an important part in
general). The series' symmetrical properties (for this more
objective piece just as the somewhat mathematical form of
this series) are used. For example fourths and fifths:
1st–3rd, 5th–6th, 12th–10th, 9th–11th notes=fifths.

Form of this movement: binary (?): exposition (bars 1–35)
and reprise (bars 36–39). Exposition: main idea (1–12),
bridge (12–22), subsidiary group (23–32), closing group (33–
35). Reprise: main group (36–48), bridge (49–52), subsidiary
group (53–61), closing group (62–69).

II *Andante amoroso* (Rondo)
a (bars 1–15, 6/8 time, Tempo I), b=first subsidiary group
(16–40, transitional from 36 on, 3/8 time, Tempo II), a (41–
55), c=second subsidiary group (56–80, 2/8 time, Tempo III).
Reprise (in the manner of a development): 'a' abbreviated and
varied (81–93, 91 already has the character of 'b', b (94–104),
c (105–142, in duet with 'b'; 'a' enters as well at bar 114, *pp*;
around 131 'a' gets more and more penetrating, and establishes
itself at 143 (beginning of the coda).

Connection with the first movement: by means of the series:
A-flat G E-flat A B-flat F C E F-sharp B C-sharp D (although two notes—C and A—have already changed places).

III *Allegro misterioso* (scherzo form and Trio: A1–B–A2, A2
being a shortened version of A1 backwards)
A1 and A2 are strictly twelve-note. Series in the same form
as second movement, which provides the connection. A (1–69)
rises chromatically to the Trio *estatico* (70–92). At the same
time this is the exposition of the fourth movement.

IV *Adagio appassionato*
Thematically connected with the Trio of the third movement.
Correspondences: IV/1 and III/74–75 viola; IV/12–13 and
III/70–73; IV/21–23 and III/81–83; IV/second half of 32–33
and III/80; IV/34–39 and III/86–92. Quotation from Alexander von Zemlinsky's 'Lyric Symphony' (completed in 1923
and published in 1926): second half of 32–33 viola and 46–50
second violin. The quotation is heard in Zemlinsky's work in
the third part of the symphony to the baritone soloist's words
'Du bist mein Eigen, mein Eigen . . .' ('You are my own, my
own . . .') taken from a poem by Rabindranath Tagore.

V *Presto delirando*
Form: A1 (1–50)—B1 (51–120)—A2 (121–211)—B2 (212–
325)—A3 (326 440)—coda (441–460).
Five-bar groups almost throughout, particularly in the Trios
B1 and B2. A is free, B is twelve-note system, based on the
series or its inversion. The form of the series in the two Trios B
is the same as that which underlies the sixth movement. It is
obtained from the third movement series by re-positioning and
runs: D-flat C A flat D F A E B-flat B D-sharp F-sharp G.

VI *Largo desolato*
Form: cantabile throughout.
The whole material of this movement, including the tonal
material (triads, etc.) and the motif from *Tristan und Isolde*
(bars 26–27, beginning of the prelude to Act I) proceeds
strictly from the twelve-note series. The following four serial
forms are used (including transpositions):
F E C F-sharp A C-sharp G-sharp D E-flat G B-flat B
(series of the Trios in the fifth movement, starting on F).
F G-flat B-flat E C-sharp A D A-flat G E-flat C B (inversion).
F F-sharp A G-sharp B-flat B/E C C-sharp D E-flat G
(half-series obtained from the series).

F E C‑sharp D C B/F‑sharp A‑sharp A G‑sharp G E‑flat (half‑series obtained from the inversion).

The similarity of these four serial forms is exploited.

Connection with the first movement: the following corres‑ pondences in particular: VI/37 and 39, and 1/5–6 or 38–39.

DER WEIN: CONCERT ARIA WITH ORCHESTRA

In the spring of 1921 Berg was commissioned by the soprano Ružena Herlinger to write a Concert Aria for her; the performing rights were to be hers alone for the first two years. *Der Wein* was written in the months May to August 1929, and it was premièred (interpreted by Mrs Herlinger, under the direction of Hermann Scherchen) on 5th June 1930 at the *Tonkünstler* Festival of the *Allgemeinen Deutschen Musikverein* in Königsberg. Berg commissioned me to write an introduction to the work; he wrote out the musical examples himself (see facsimile). My note won his approval and was printed in the programme. The following is a reprint of that note, shortened by the omission of the biographical dates and dates of compositions.

The textual foundation of the Aria is three poems by Baudelaire in Stefan George's German translation: 'Die Seele des Weines' ('The soul of the wine'), 'Der Wein der Liebenden' ('The wine of lovers') and 'Der Wein der Einsamen' ('The wine of the lonely'). In the first poem the wine's voice directs the poet to lay himself open to the joys and sufferings of mankind. The wine's 'soul' is here interpreted as its power to bring men together. The wine's inherent faculty for raising the individual out of himself, and making him grow and achieve a certain identity with the experience of love—this is the content of the middle section, which tells of a flight into eternity *à deux* on the wings of wine. Wine as solace of the lonely, and redeemer of man's fearfulness in the face of his likeness to God—this is the end of the trilogy, and brings us back to the mood of the opening.

The Aria lasts about fifteen minutes and uses a relatively small but very colourful orchestra. It is introduced musically by an instrumental prelude in which a slinking figure in the bass under dull, sustained wind chords interprets the fermentation of the wine in the vat. Passages of fourths initiate a gradual transition to the main theme, whose calm lines accompany the wine's soul's appeal. The musical evolution is enlivened at the mention of the refreshing effect of the grape-juice. Brass shapes like 'breaks' build up the tension, and a 'tempo di tango'— with the characteristic fourths in the accompanying piano and the corresponding melancholy of sixths in the saxophone solo— leads into the description of the aphrodisiac effect of wine. The middle section is reached via a very expressive 'molto acceler-ando'; it begins 'slightly restless' and reflects the really erotic experience of intoxication in the most delicate colours—

'floatingly' almost throughout. After the strings have breathed their last *ppp*, there comes a postlude that develops two earlier sections in retrograde (bars 152–159 correspond to 123–130, and 160–167 to 115–122). This forms the bridge into the third part, which takes up the theme of the orchestral introduction. The individual reflections of the lonely one are shaped in a manner rich in references, by means of reminiscences from the corresponding passages in the first part. A powerful uprising of the full orchestra followed by a gradual fadeout ends the Aria with a sort of coda.

All the musical events of the work are derived from a twelvenote series. The basic shape is: B A Gsharp Fsharp E Eflat C G F Dflat D Bflat. This serial shape proves extraordinarily favourable for the formation of a vocal form of cantabile lines. The scale sequence of the series' first half furthers the production of such lines and the construction of chords made up of thirds. The absence of augmented and diminished intervals increases the singability of the vocal part—a part that makes enormous demands on the interpreter, not only purely musically, but also as regards the matter of spiritual empathy with the work. Incidentally Berg did not want the Aria to be performed exclusively by sopranos. He frequently expressed the desire to hear it sung by a tenor. (Unfortunately this desire was not satisfied in his lifetime.)

LULU

The following appreciation of the opera was undertaken in response to American publication demands; these led Berg to discuss the work (in short score) with me in detail over many days in 1934. Many passages of the text and most of the musical examples stem from him.

There is a remarkable analogy between the choice of *Wozzeck* and the decision to set Frank Wedekind's *Lulu* tragedy. In both cases it was a dramatic performance that presented the material in concrete form to the artist's view. The impression made on him by Karl Kraus's production of 'Pandora's Box' in Vienna on 29th May 1905 was reinforced by Kraus's speech at the première, which he published shortly afterwards in his magazine 'Die Fackel' (No. 182, 9th June 1905).[17] Berg noted down parts of this speech at the time; the first line of the passages quoted below reappeared in his birthday dedication to Karl Kraus in 1934.

Since Berg identified himself completely with the conception of the *Lulu* tragedy contained in Kraus's speech, it seems relevant to insert here a few passages from that speech:

' "A soul rubbing the sleep from her eyes in paradise." A poet and lover, vacillating between love and the artistic design of the beauty of woman, holds Lulu's hand in his and utters words that are the key to this maze of femininity, to this labyrinth in which many a man lost track of his reason. It is the last act of *Erdgeist*. The mistress of love has gathered all types of manhood around her, so that they can serve her by taking what she has to offer. Alwa, her husband's son, puts it into words. And then, when he has drunk himself full at this sweet spring of corruption, when his fate has been fulfilled, he will find the words, in the last act of *Büchse der Pandora*, in delirium before the portrait of Lulu: 'In front of this portrait I retrieve my self-respect. It makes my doom comprehensible to me. All we have been through is so natural, so obvious, so clear as sunlight. Whoever feels secure in his respectability in the face of these blooming, swelling lips, these great child's eyes, full of inno-cence, this rosy white, exuberant body, let him throw the first stone at us." These words, spoken before the picture of the woman *who became the destroyer of all because everyone destroyed her,* encompass the world of the poet Frank Wedekind.' [Author's italics.]

'. . . And then the mighty double tragedy, . . . *the tragedy of the hounded grace of woman, eternally misunderstood,* who is per-mitted merely to climb into the Procrustean bed of the moral concepts of a stingy world. Woman is made to run the gauntlet; Woman who was never intended by her creator to serve the egoism of her proprietors, and who can rise to her higher values only in freedom.'

'One of the dramatic conflicts between female nature and some male blockhead placed Lulu in the hands of terrestrial justice, and she would have had nine years in prison in which to reflect that beauty is a punishment from God, had not her devoted slaves of love hatched a romantic plan for her libera-tion, a plan that could never ripen in the real world even in the most fanatical brain, and that the most fanatical will could never bring to fruition. But *Büchse der Pandora* opens with Lulu's liberation—with the success of the impossible the poet delineates the love-slaves' capacity for sacrifice far better than he could have done by the introduction of some more credible motif. Lulu, who carried the action forward in *Erdgeist*, now has to be carried along by the action. Now more than before it becomes apparent that it is her grace that is the actual suffering heroine of the drama; her portrait, the image of her best days, now plays a larger part than she herself, and whereas earlier it was her active charms that motivated the action, now—at every station on the road of suffering—it is the discrepancy between her former magnificence and her present woe that arouses our feelings. The great retribution has begun, the revenge of a world of men which makes bold to avenge itself for its own guilt.'

'In a loose series of events such as might have been invented by some cheap thriller-writer, the clear eyes sees the construc-tion of a world of perspectives, moods and jolting emotions; and "back stairs poetry" becomes a real poetry of the back stairs which can only be condemned by that sort of official weak-mindedness which prefers a badly painted palace to a well painted gutter. But the truth is not to be found on such a stage, but behind it. In Wedekind's world, where men live for the sake of thought, there is little room for circumstantial realism! He is the first German dramatist to reinstate thought— lacking for so long—on the stage. The whole whimsy of naturalism is as if blown away. *What lies above and below a man is more important than what dialect he speaks.*'

'These outrageous proceedings may be repellent to anyone who asks nothing more from art than relaxation, or that it should not overstep the limits of his own capacity for suffering. But his judgment would have to be just as weak as his nerves if he would deny the greatness of this design. Realistic expecta-tions with regard to this fevered vision in a London attic are just as misplaced as they were with regard to the "improbable" liberation in Act I and the disposal of Rodrigo in Act II. And whoever sees this sequence of four customers coming to Lulu in her final status as a prostitute merely as a raw piece of spice, and cannot see this exchange of grotesque and tragic impressions—this pile-up of frightful visages—as the inspiration of a poet, should not complain about the low estimation of his own capacity for experience.'

'But it is impossible in all seriousness to believe that anyone could be so shortsighted as to mistake—on account of the "embarrassing" stuff of the drama—the greatness of the treat-ment and the inner necessity in the choice of this "stuff". To overlook,—blinded by the truncheons, revolvers and daggers— the fact that this sex-murder is like a doom brought up from the deepest depths of Woman's nature; to forget—on account of this Countess Geschwitz's Lesbian disposition—that she has greatness and is not just any pathological creature, but stalks through the tragedy like a demon of un-pleasure.'

'The objection that some one has "put something into" a piece of writing would be the highest praise. For only in dramas whose floor is just below their ceiling is it impossible, even with the best will in the world, to put anything into them. But into the true work of art, in which a poet has shaped his world, everyone can put everything. What happens in *Büchse der Pandora* can be brought to bear as much on our aesthetic atti- tude as—hear, hear!—on our moralistic attitude to Woman. The question as to whether the poet is more concerned with the joy of her blooming or with the contemplation of her ruinous career is one that each can answer as he pleases.'

To supplement these passages we may introduce a passage written by a critic after the first performance of the Lulu Sym- phony in Prague in January 1935. Berg attached great value to it as being a particularly succinct formulation—conjuring up the mythical essence of the character of Lulu—of his own point of view. 'Lulu is a heroine of super-dimensional power in ex- periencing and suffering; destroying everything around her that succumbs to her charms or even approaches her, she is a piece of Nature beyond good and evil, and therefore—as a complete, closed cosmos on her own—only to be unravelled by means of music, in a context removed from all conceptual thought. The way this glowing fireball—singeing everything that comes in contact with her—is finally herself extinguished presented a challenge to the psychologist in the musician, a challenge to come to terms with that unreal sphere where dream images like figures flit past into death, just because in dying they are struck once more by the last rays from some great innocent demon. After Alban Berg's *Wozzeck*, his *Lulu* will live on for ever; she has it easier than poor Wozzeck, for with Don Juan and Faust she is one of those who is constantly reincarnated amongst us changing shapes, and has only to catch a poet's glance, not be formed by him out of nothing.' The reference to Don Juan touched Berg especially, as he himself liked to regard Lulu as the female counterpart of that figure.

Berg arranged the Wedekind text according to principles quite different from those he had applied to *Wozzeck*. In the earlier opera he had to obtain a taut dramatic structure by means of re-ordering and condensing a few scenes; whereas the action in Wedekind's tragedy is already very taut and Berg's job was rather to shorten the all too extensive dialogue for the purpose of setting it to music, without altering the sequence of events. Further, he had to find a way of combining the two pieces *Erdgeist* and *Büchse der Pandora*. Berg shortened the text by omitting many conversations of a reflective kind; and by including a short film intermezzo he managed to unite the last act of *Erdgeist* and the first act of *Büchse der Pandora* into the central act of a three-act opera.

In *Wozzeck* the many short scenes were quite closed and complete as regards their content and character and this suggested a musical formation that would preserve the particular design of each individual scene. Hence the selection of 'character pieces' based on the forms of instrumental music. Here, on the other hand, the important thing was to represent a development of the human characters. Thus the first important element in the musical design was the human voice; the general preference for the vocal forms (arias, recitatives, ensembles) is supplemented by an exhaustive exploitation of all the technical possibilities of the vocal material. The constant alternation between all conceivable varieties of speech and song is a particular characteristic of this opera. The frequent coloratura passages in Lulu's part are supposed to hint—by stylization—at that unreal sphere in which the heroine of the opera—'Night changeling of love' as Kraus called her—moves with dream-like virtuosity. It is also profoundly significant that Berg had the male parts that cause Lulu's deepest humiliation in the last scene sung by the singers who had previously played the characters who met their deaths through Lulu (Public Health Officer Goll,

25   Death Mask, taken by Anna Mahler

26, 27   Première of *Lulu* at the Zürich Stadttheater on 2nd June 1937

Painter Schwarz, Dr Schön). This represents a primary expression, merely with the character of the voices, or 'the revenge
of a world of men that makes bold to avenge itself for its own
guilt'.

The orchestra—which requires only triple winds (as opposed
to *Wozzeck*), but makes extensive use of piano and vibraphone
—also has important symbolic functions: some of the characters (e.g. Rodrigo and Schigolch) are characterized by a particular instrumental colouring that is consistently maintained
throughout the work. By altering dynamics and orchestration,
passages that are thematically identical acquire a completely
new colour. The distinction between the accompanying and
dominating functions of the orchestra is much more strictly
executed than in *Wozzeck*. The highest law of reproduction
must be the working out of the vocal line which runs through
the whole opera; Berg facilitated this by instrumentation of
unexampled transparency.

In *Wozzeck* the character of the individual scenes was largely
responsible for determining the musical forms in the work; in
Lulu the character—'the total phenomenon to be put across'
(Berg)—of each of the stage figures (much more broadly presented in this case) was determinant for the musical construction. This will become quite clear when we come to discuss
the individual scenes, but as an example of the way the human
characters on the stage determine the musical orientation we
may mention here that Sonata form was selected for the appearance of Dr Schön, Rondo form for Alwa, and the exotic
pentatonic music for the Countess Geschwitz. Naturally Berg
also used every opportunity provided by the text to create
symmetry, musical lucidity and compactness; we may mention
in this connection the symmetrical construction of the whole of
Act II, and the Society scene in Act III that is distributed
between three large ensembles.

The work's thematic unity is guaranteed by the fact that a
single twelve-note series—allotted to Lulu—determines the
whole musical action of the opera (example 11). Berg used

special methods to derive all the most important musical figures from this series, as is shown in the few examples that follow. Quite generally we may remark that in this work, as in the *Lyric Suite* and *Der Wein*, Berg uses the twelve-note technique in a highly specific manner that is specially adaptable—besides the exercise of its purely musical function—to the particular needs of the music dramatist. So he manages to refer the whole 'leitmotivic' and 'leit-harmonic' structure of his opera to a single musical figure, just as the poet placed a single human figure at the centre of his drama; everything else is 'produced' from her and stands in a functional relationship to her.

Example 12 shows how a motif of four three-part chords is derived from the basic series; this motif is associated with the portrait of Lulu which plays a significant part in the work.

Example 13 shows how a scale-wise shape is obtained from these 'portrait harmonies'; with a dancing rhythm this provides an important Lulu theme (example 14). By a variety of simple

procedures other series are derived from the basic series. By taking every seventh note of the original series one obtains the

series of example 15. This series is allotted to Alwa and becomes the theme of his Rondo (example 16). The theme has a
pronounced 'minor key' flavour, well suited to the elegiac
character of Alwa.

The series of example 17 is obtained by taking every fifth
note of the original series. Example 18 shows how, with the

open fifth G–D sustained, this series determines the pentatonic
music allotted to the Countess Geschwitz.

Another simple procedure is adopted for obtaining the series
allotted to Dr Schön (example 19). The main theme of Dr

Schön's Sonata consists of this series (example 20); in accordance with Schön's masterful character it has a distinct 'major key' flavour.

Another method is used to obtain a motif of fourths from the basic series; this is the 'Erdgeist theme' that runs through the whole opera (example 21). The 'waste product', or series

consisting of the remaining eight notes, is also introduced in the course of the musical development in its original and retrograde forms and their inversions. (The same applies to most of the other figures given in these examples.)

Berg himself notated (with headings) the formal sense of the most important passages in the opera, and these have been retained by Erwin Stein in his vocal score. So here we need only make a few supplementary remarks in addition to Berg's own notes. But let it be noted that we cannot here demonstrate *all* the thematic relationships; these are after all guaranteed by the consistent application of the twelve-note technique. We can only indicate such relationships when it is a matter of demonstrating their function with regard to the dramatic events or the formal construction.

ACT I [The bar numbers in the first two acts are from the vocal score, those in Act III from Berg's short score.]
The piece opens with the 'Erdgeist fourths' of example 21.
The Animal Tamer's prologue in front of the curtain (the last

part of the opera to be composed) derives its musical form from the treatment of the voice, which grows from spoken, with bass drum roll, through melodramatic expression as in Schönberg's *Pierrot Lunaire*, 'half-sung' rubato, sung parlando, to the full entry of the singing voice, and then back in reverse order. The presentation of the animals is used for the exposition of the themes of some of the main characters of the opera. The tiger (bar 21 ff.) brings Dr Schön's theme; the piano tone-clusters (bar 16) characterize the 'bear' Rodrigo; the 'snake' Lulu is introduced by the scale-wise vocal theme belonging to her, etc.

The first scene is played in painter Schwarz's studio, and consists of a loose series of little pieces. The introductory recitative conversation is followed in bar 132 by a 'poco Adagio' duet between Lulu and the painter which may be regarded as an 'Introduction' to the canon that accompanies his pursuit of Lulu. The 'portrait harmonies' of example 12 are thematically important in this passage; they appear for the first time in bar 132. The canon itself is dominated by Lulu's scale theme (example 14) derived from the portrait harmonies. The coda leads back to the 'poco Adagio' of the opening. The entry of the Public Health Officer is treated briefly, breathlessly and melodramatically. Lulu's monologue over his corpse is in the form of a 'Canzonetta'. The bridge to the next scene collects these little pieces together in an animated develop-ment movement.

In the second scene too the music grows out of the spoken dialogue. The little duet between Lulu and the painter is recapitulated by the orchestra (from bar 438) as a sort of 'second verse'. The entry of Schigolch introduces the chromati-cism characteristic of this scurrilous character; its derivation from the basic series can be studied in example 22. A special chamber music colouring is also allotted to this character and maintained throughout the opera; on this occasion the instru-ments are nine woodwinds and pizzicato strings. With Dr Schön's entry his 'Sonata' begins; the individual sections are as follows: bar 533 the energetic idea for strings—a main theme

corresponding to this 'man of power'; bar 554 the transitional group; bar 561 the subsidiary theme constructed like a grand⁄fatherly Gavotte, symbolizing Schön's longing for orderly, bourgeois conditions; bar 615 the melodramatic coda to Lulu's words expressing her profound attachment to Schön. The reprise of the exposition begins in bar 625 and follows exactly the repeated sequence of conversational topics; at its climax (bar 666), just where the coda enters, it is interrupted by a new form—'monoritmica'—adapted to the changing scenic events. The ascent of this form (bars 666–842) accompanies Schön's communications with the painter and the latter's suicide, and the descent (843–956) accompanies the argument between Dr Schön, Alwa and Lulu. The monoritmica represents the de⁄velopment of the rhythm given in example 23, from Grave to

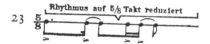

Prestissimo and back to Grave. The accelerando is executed with eighteen fixed changes of tempo one after another, whereas the ritardando is a gradual one. The monoritmica is followed directly (bar 957) by the interrupted coda of the composed repeat of the Sonata exposition. This, much more broadly executed than before, dominates the whole of the interlude and is replaced in bar 992 by the Ragtime played by the jazzband backstage.

The Ragtime forms the basis of the melodrama that opens the third scene. The voice part begins with Lulu's entry. Alwa, 'almost painfully blinded' by the sight of Lulu, clutches his heart; in the orchestra we hear his Rondo theme for the first time (bar 1021). The conversation between Lulu and Alwa begins Arioso, but soon evolves into a melodrama, accom' panied by the jazzband's English Waltz (bar 1040). Alwa remains alone with a recitative; his words 'Über die liesse sich freilich eine interessante Oper schreiben' ('An interesting opera could be written about her') (bar 1095 ff.) are accompanied by the quotation from the beginning of *Wozzeck*. The appearance of the Prince introduces a musical form that also occurs in the other acts associated with two other merely episodic characters. It is a Chorale with concertante decoration by one of the solo strings—here the cello; the room servant in Act II is allotted the viola; the pimp in Act III the violin. The bars (1113– 1122) preceding the working of the Chorale represent a sort of harmonic exposition of the cello solo. The confusion caused by Lulu fainting is accompanied by fragments of the introductory Ragtime. At Dr Schön's entry the voices unite in a powerful, sustained sextet accompanied by four solo strings. This is laid out in mirror form around the pause in bar 1190. The big conversation between Lulu and Dr Schön which ends the first act represents musically the development and the last reprise (from bar 1289) of the Schön Sonata. The subsidiary theme Gavotte is worked out into a 'letter duet'. Schön's collapse is followed by the coda, condensed into six bars.

ACT II
This act begins with a recitative-like conversation scene; Geschwitz's pentatonic music dominates the accompaniment. Dr Schön's monologue 'Das mein Lebensabend . . .' ('The evening of my life . . .') is arioso in style; a motif derived from the main theme of his Sonata is used as an ostinato in the bass, and reappears on later occasions when Schön's persecution mania gets the upper hand. Lulu's conversation with Schön is similar to the analogous situation in Act I, scene 2 (the Duettino between Lulu and the painter); this time the form is a Cavatina for Lulu with recitative interjections by Schön. The

entry of Schigolch, Rodrigo and the schoolboy produces an ensemble constructed on Schigolch's chromaticism, Rodrigo's coarse piano chords and the fanfare-like themes of the school-boy. The music of Lulu's brief appearance (bars 145–172) corresponds to the introduction of Alwa's Rondo (Alwa is after all the expected one that Lulu is talking about). A three-part canon and renewed ensemble follows until the room ser-vant announces Alwa's arrival. This announcement introduces another Chorale episode, this time with concertante viola. At bar 243 the Rondo begins, again growing out of the spoken word; this 'symphonic movement' includes both the delicate and passionate love scenes in the opera. Berg once characterized the Rondo with the motto: 'As the artist sees Lulu, and as she must be seen so that one can understand that—despite all the frightful things that come about because of her—she is so beloved.' So the Rondo, whose first part dies softly away at bar 336, has become the lyrical main piece of the whole work, the proclamation—in the centre of the opera—of Berg's especial affection for his last operatic figure, who was to illuminate even the fevered fantasies of his last hours.

The following tumultuoso is dominated by the motif of Schön's persecution mania. The Rondo theme and the Rod-rigo chords (broken up into semiquavers) are sounded. Schön's great outburst is designed as an Aria with five verses, interrupted by Lulu's brief interjections accompanied by her themes. Before the last verse Berg has placed Lulu's fundamental confession of faith; this 'colaratura Lied' 'in the tempo of the pulse-beat' exposes her innermost essence, completely lost to the sphere of morality:

> *If people have killed themselves for my sake,*
> *   that doesn't detract from my value.*
> *You knew why you were taking me for a wife*
> *   just as well as I knew why I was taking you for a husband.*
> *You had betrayed your best friends with me;*
> *   you couldn't very well go on and betray yourself with me too.*
> *If you are bringing me the whole evening of your life as a sacrifice,*
> *   at least you have had the whole of my youth in exchange.*

*I never in the world wanted to seem anything other
than what people took me for.
And never in the world has anyone taken me for anything other
than what I am.*

The whole is set for the freest 'vacillating' type of vocal delivery;
the orchestra performs a purely accompanying function, and
only takes over the vocal line in the postlude. The main rhythm
of example 23 drones out at the murder of Schön. From bar 587
Schön's series (example 19) gradually resolves back into the main
series of the opera, which is played by the orchestra in unison in
bars 603–604. Textually and thematically, Lulu's Arietta after
Schön's death corresponds to a large degree with her Canzonetta
after the death of the Public Health Officer in Act I.

With Lulu's arrest impending, an orchestral interlude
('Ostinato') is introduced with the curtain closed; all the serial
shapes that occur in the opera are brought up through a tumultuous build-up of ostinato semiquaver figures to a climax in
bar 680. A bridge leads to a peaceful middle section (bars
685–689) based on the 'Erdgeist fourths' and the 'portrait
motif'. From the middle of bar 687 the music runs in the
opposite direction (exactly in all its parts). But the general
character of the piece, which is in many respects the orchestral
counterpart of the 'Allegro misterioso' in the Lyric Suite, is
completely darkened in the retrograde part by a general muting.
This is in keeping with the relevance of this piece to the
dramatic development. Berg earmarked this music to accompany a film sequence that was to establish the connection between Wedekind's two dramas, and indicate the reverse of
fortune that overtakes the heroine.[18] Lulu, after her fabulous
ascent to the peak of social position, has become the murderer
—in a very adventurous manner—of her husband; she is
arrested, condemned and, after a year in prison, liberated in an
equally adventurous manner. The second scene shows the
beginning of her catastrophic fall.

In his libretto book Berg gave the following indications as to
the layout of the film sequence that was to accompany the

Ostinato: During the transitional music a silent film is to indicate the course of Lulu's fortunes in the next years. The film sequence—in accordance with the symmetrical course of the music—should also be quasi-symmetrical (i.e. it should run forwards and then backwards). To this end the events that correspond, together with their accompanying phenomena, should be fitted together as closely as possible.[19] This gives us the following series of scenes (following the direction of the arrows):

Arrest	*En route to her final liberation* ↑
The three people concerned in the arrest	The three people involved in the liberation
Lulu in chains	Lulu at liberty (disguised as the Countess Geschwitz)
Detention pending trial	*Isolation ward*
Nervous expectancy	Nervous expectancy
Her hopes disappearing	Growing hopes
Trial	*Medical council*
Her guilt	The illness
Judge and jury	Doctor and students
The three witnesses	The three helpers in the
The judgment	liberation
Her transfer in the Black	Her transfer in the
Maria to the	ambulance from the
Prison	*Prison*
The prison door shuts	The prison door opens
Initial resignation	Awakening will to live
Lulu's portrait—as a	Lulu's portrait—as a
shadow on the prison wall	reflection in a shovel

↓ ————————→ *One year's imprisonment* ————————→

For the second scene the curtain rises on the same room in which the first scene of this act took place; but Berg expressly requires 'a dead, dusty, uninhabited feeling in the room in contrast to the preceding scene. The room is carefully shuttered against the daylight outside.' Recitative and spoken dialogue are used up to bar 787. Schigolch's entry introduces a Largo (bar 789) which is a 'slow motion', note-for-note repeat of the ensemble of bars 94–120 in this act, which goes about twice as fast. After a short interruption of recitative and dialogue the schoolboy's entry (bar 834) brings in a 'chamber music' of winds, piano and eight solo strings which develops the earlier fanfares in lively 9/8 movement, shadowy and swift. The following melodrama that accompanies Lulu's appearance is another 'slow motion' passage corresponding to the music of her appearance in the first part of this act (from 145); this leads into the continuation of the Rondo. This runs from 1001–1096 and accompanies a repetition of the scenic action in the corresponding passage in the first part. Alwa's glowing hymn, with the orchestra rushing up like a giant harp, closes this act with one last triumph for Lulu.

ACT III

The great Society scene that begins this act has a very special position in the whole of Berg's operatic music because it is the only occasion when his work leans definitely towards surrealism. The false brilliance that had to be created here produced a music that took long stretches of its sound from a world of illusion; the orchestrion [a sort of 'mechanical orchestra' in the form of an organ, invented 1851] of the circus tents sets the tone, equating falsity and brilliance. This becomes clear in the three big ensembles that make up the scene and include various smaller forms within them. A note in the score qualifies the mood and declamatory tone of these ensembles:

1. Listless—parlando
2. Festive—cantato
3. Excited—spoken

Only a few of the main voices are to be prominent in the first twelve-part ensemble; the rest are submerged in the general murmuring and the unremitting orchestral accompaniment.

Lulu's great argument with Casti Piani is set, in analogy to the previous acts, to concertante Chorale variations; here the solo violin is the obligato allotted to the character of the pimp. The Chorale theme is intoned by the cello in bars 83–88, and reappears in the second variation as horn chords. At bar 103 the chain of variations is interrupted by two intermezzi: to Casti Piani's words 'Von den unzähligen Abenteuerinnen ...' ('Of the numberless adventuresses ...') we hear the solo violin play a melody set by Wedekind to one of his *Lautenlieder*[20] (example 24), the theme of the later variation movement that constitutes the connection between the two scenes in this act.

24

Lulu's decided refusal to be sold to a brothel by Casti Piani has an instrumental accompaniment from bar 119 consisting of her coloratura song from Act II distributed between soloistic woodwinds and brass. At bar 146 the Chorale variations proceed, and follow the individual turns of conversation in quick succession up until Lulu's outburst: 'Du kannst mich nicht ausliefern!' ('You can't hand me over!') in the twelfth variation, which closes the cycle with a stretto. An important detail: bars 212–222 with Lulu's words 'Aber ich kann nicht das Einzige verkaufen, was je mein eigen war' ('But I can't sell the only thing that was ever my own') correspond exactly with the analogous passage in Act II after the murder of Dr Schön (bars 635–645).

The following ensemble is the last part of the opera instru‐ mented by Berg himself (ending at bar 268). He had orches‐ trated the variations movement and parts of the last scene much earlier for the Symphonic Pieces. In this ensemble three pages are left empty in the original score after bar 260, with a note by Berg: 'Insertion of 22 bars for the possible extension of the ensemble and clarification of the dialogue Lulu—Geschwitz'.

The following conversation between Rodrigo and Lulu is dominated by piano themes of Rodrigo and Geschwitz's pentatonic music. In the whole opera these two are treated as opposite characters. The guests' entry into the play room is accompanied by a pantomime which the music follows rhapso-dically. In the short score there is a drawing by Berg to show the movement on the stage.

Schigolch's entry introduces a hasty 'chamber music' based on his chromaticism. The argument between Rodrigo and Casti Piani takes the form of a double cadenza for violin and piano with spoken dialogue. From here on the four distinct types of delivery—spoken, recitative, parlando, cantato—are constantly alternating; their analogous sequence alone produces three little forms that correspond to the conversations Rodrigo –Lulu, Lulu–Geschwitz, and Geshwitz–Rodrigo.

The third ensemble, which brings the financial collapse of almost everybody present ('The whole world is losing') is a sort of inversion of the earlier one ('The whole world is gaining'). Lulu's flight is accompanied by sparing recitative. While the Groom in Lulu's clothes is idling in front of Lulu's portrait we hear the 'portrait motif'; the appearance of Casti Piani occasions another brief entry of the solo violin. Just as the substitution is noticed and the Groom threatens to break out into wild laughter, the curtain falls quickly into the first bar of the transitional music.

Casti Piani's ballad forms the basis of the transitional music. In the course of the piece this ballad goes through the follow-ing changes of musical character—though the melody is always repeated note-for-note—and the following build-up from varia-tion to variation:

The first variation (Maestoso, in the 3/4 time of the theme) opens purely tonally (C major) and is instrumentated with pomp and splendour. The circus orchestrion-sound refers back to the false brilliance and cheating grandeur of the preceding scene in the *demi-monde*. The second variation (Grazioso in 4/4 time) is intended to show Lulu's response to that world (polytonal); even the brutality of the whole sphere is gracefully transformed by her temperament. By contrast, the third variation (Funèbre, 5/4 time) deals with a further station on her road of suffering—Alwa's supreme sacrifice (tonality completely dissolved). At last in the fourth variation (Affettuoso, 7/4 time), using the means of the twelve-note technique, the climax of the great emotional build-up of this interlude is reached. Only now do we hear an indication of the theme of the variations in its original harmonic and rhythmic form: it comes up from the alley as if played by a barrel organ and enters Lulu's miserable attic, the scene of her deepest humiliation.

The string tremolo on the A major triad which 'drums up the parade' and represents the rain accompanies the cynical conversation of Alwa and Schigolch with which the scene begins. The tonal area conjures up the musical character of Dr Schön. Sung dialogue begins with Lulu's entrance. From this point on the music represents a 'composed ritardando' that passes through the following stages: Presto, Vivace, Allegro, Animato, Allegretto, Andantino, Sostenuto, Andante, Adagio, Lento, Largo, Grave, and the transitions are precisely regulated with metronome indications.

The themes of Lulu's first guest are largely related with the music that accompanied the appearance of the Public Health Officer in Act I, scene 1. Against the melodramatic conversation between Schigolch and Alwa we hear again the ballad on the barrel organ, accompanied by the 'rain tremolo'. Geschwitz's entry brings back her pentatonic music and the 'portrait harmonies'; Alwa's lyrical outburst at sight of the portrait repeats the 'Hymn' from Act II, and later the other voices join him in a little quartet. The intervention of Geschwitz, who wants to prevent Lulu from going out onto the street again, introduces a very changed repetition of the fourth variation from the interlude. Alwa and Schigolch left alone, we hear—

Welturaufführung

LULU

von Alban Berg
nach den Tragödien „Erdgeist" und „Büchse der
Pandora" von Frank Wedekind

Musikleitung	Robert F. Denzler
Spielleitung	Karl Schmid-Bloss
Bühnenbild	Roman Clemens
Korrepetition	Willy Häusslein und Jngolf Marcus
Kostüme	Jürg Stockar

Personen

Lulu . . . . Nuri Hadzic a.G.
Gräfin Geschwitz . . . . Maria Bernhard
Eine Theatergarderobière . . . . Frieda Kurz
Ein Gymnasiast . . . . Erika Feichtinger a.G.
Der Medizinalrat . . . . Karl Melzer
Der Maler . . . . Paul Feher
Dr. Schön, Chefredakteur . . . . Asger Stig
Alwa, Dr. Schön's Sohn, Schriftsteller . . . . . Peter Baxevanos
Ein Tierbändiger . . }
Rodrigo, ein Athlet . } . . . . Albert Emmerich
Schigolch, ein Greis . . . . Fritz Honisch
Der Prinz, ein Afrikareisender . . . . Oscar Mörwald
Der Theaterdirektor . . . . Walter Frank
Ein Kammerdiener . . . . Peter Pöschl a.G.

I. Akt	1. Szene: Ein Maleratelier, 2. Szene: Ein eleganter Salon
	3. Szene: Eine Theatergarderobe
II. Akt	1. und 2. Szene: Ein grosser Saal in deutscher Renaissance

---

Pause nach dem 1. Akt

Der Film im 2. Akt wurde unter der Regie von Heinz Rückert
von der Firma Hans Rudolf Meyer „Tempo" Zürich gedreht

almost note-for-note—the second variation, the 'rain tremolo' forming the bridge to Lulu's entry with the Negro. The music of this passage is an abbreviated repeat of the 'monoritmica' in Act I. The 'rain tremolo' again provides the bridge passage. Schigolch and the corpse of Alwa; repeat of the third variation —the 'Funèbre' discloses its real significance only now. Geschwitz and Schigolch alone; the pentatonic music har- monized with open fifths—the 'rain tremolo' is transformed into Schigolch's chromaticism. Lulu enters with Jack the Ripper; the music takes up the Dr Schön themes; bars 1194–1204 contain a reference to the Cavatina in Act II. When Lulu says 'Was starren Sie mich auf einmal so an?' ('Why are you suddenly staring at me like that?') the coda of the 'Sonata' begins.

The last part of the tragedy begins with Geschwitz's mono- logue (bar 1253, Lento) which is marked 'Nocturno' in the short score. Lulu's dying shriek, with indescribably strident instrumentation, floods the stage once more with all the horror of these last moments, and then, in the elegy of the dying friend, Berg gives expression to that mourning, far removed from all earthly things, over all the ties that run through this ghostly night-piece, ties that occasioned so much passion, so much suffering: 'Lulu! My angel! Show yourself once more! I am close! will stay close to you—in eternity!' As these words dis- engage themselves from the orchestral sound like dark shadows and reverberate away, there sounds a delicate reminiscence from *Wozzeck*: Marie's open fifths in an A minor chord, the motif of her futile waiting. The opera ends with the incorporation of these fifths in Lulu's series.

With the exception of a few bars, *Lulu* is complete in the short score. The voice parts are finished, and the orchestral part is also notated with skeleton instrumental indications except for two or three staves. The full score of Act III breaks off at bar 268, at the end of the second ensemble of the Society scene. Bars 1120–1161 and 1268–1300 of Act III were also orches- trated for the Adagio of the Lulu Symphony.

28 (*above*)   The second production of *Lulu* at the Zurich Stadttheater in 1963
29 (*below*)   *Lulu* at the festival performance of the Theater an der Wien, 1962-3

30, 31 Performances of *Wozzeck* on 5th March 1929 at the Landestheater, Oldenburg (*above*), and in Berlin in 1961 (*below*)

Berg dedicated Lulu's coloratura song in Act II in the autumn of 1933 to Anton von Webern on his fiftieth birthday; he wrote this dedication in the full score and the vocal score. The whole opera he dedicated to Arnold Schönberg with the following words:[21]

My dearest friend!

I know that in answer to my—to Alwa's question 'May I come in?' (the first words of the opera Lulu after the curtain rises) you would answer with Schön 'Just make yourself at home', and that then I would put into my embrace all the feelings that fill my soul on this 13th September.[22] That—the fact that I can only do this from a distance—is one thing that pains me this day. Another pain is that I cannot approach you with a real *present*, but only with a *dedication*. Please accept it, not only as a product of years of work earnestly undertaken for your sake, but also as a documentation of my innermost conviction, as a document for all to see. The whole world, and the German world too, shall recognize in the dedication of this German opera that it is indigenous in the sphere of the most German music, which will bear *your name* for time everlasting.

A third pain: that I cannot lay the score of the whole opera at your feet, but only a fair copy of the opening. But the formula 'to write down' applies unfortunately to *Lulu* too . . .

VIOLIN CONCERTO

The general part of the following discussion of the Concerto (from the words 'Insofar as a transcription into words is possible at all . . .') was written in con-nection with the birthday tribute to Alma Maria Mahler mentioned on page 102, both suggested and authorized by Berg himself. I wrote the analytical part in the spring of 1936 under Anton Webern's guidance.

The last work that Berg completed, the Violin Concerto, appears as an image of farewell; not only because of the tragic external circumstances but also for convincing internal musical reasons. With the incorporation of the Chorale, Berg moved into—for him—virgin formal territory; at the same time, glancing back, it represents an especially simple and trans-parent crystallization of important features of all his preceding work. J. S. Bach's Chorale 'Vor Deinen Thron tret' ich hiermit' ('Herewith I come before Thy throne'), dictated from his deathbed, Brahms' last work, the Organ Fantasia on 'O Welt ich muss dich lassen' ('O world I must leave you'), and Mahler's *Lied von der Erde* may all be interpreted as farewells in a similar sense.

Insofar as a transcription into words is possible at all, the 'tone'—a favourite expression of Berg's—of the whole work may be described as follows: delicate Andante melodies emerge from the rising and falling movement of the introduction. These crystallize into a Grazioso middle section and then dis-solve back into the waves of the opening. The Allegretto Scherzo rises from the same background; this part captures the vision of the lovely girl in a graceful dance which alternates be-tween a delicate and dreamy character and the rustic character of a Kärnten folk tune. A wild orchestral cry introduces the second main part, which begins as a free and stormy cadenza.

The demonic action moves irresistibly towards catastrophe, interrupted once—briefly—by a reserved point of rest. Groans and strident cries for help are heard in the orchestra, choked off by the suffocating rhythmic pressure of destruction. Finally: over a long pedal point—gradual collapse. At the moment of highest suspense and anxiety, the Chorale enters, serious and solemn, in the solo violin. Like an organ the woodwinds answer each verse with the original harmonization of the classical model. Ingenious variations follow, with the original Chorale melody always present as a *cantus firmus*, climbing 'misterioso' from the bass while the solo violin intones a 'plaint' that gradually struggles towards the light. The dirge grows continually in strength; the soloist, with a visible gesture, takes over the leadership of the whole body of violins and violas; gradually they all join in with his melody and rise to a mighty climax before separating back into their own parts. An in-describably melancholy reprise of the Kärnten folk tune 'as if in the distance (but much slower than the first time)' reminds us once more of the lovely image of the girl; then the Chorale, with bitter harmonies, ends this sad farewell while the solo violin arches high over it with entry after entry of the plaint.

After this 'description' one is tempted simply to relegate the Concerto to the category of 'programme music'. A closer in-spection of the formal and thematic construction shows that Berg based his 'tone poem' freshly and firmly on absolute music; the strictness and compactness of his ingenious working is in nowise inferior to the achievements of his earlier works. In its general outlines, the form of this work must have hovered in the composer's mind right from the start; details were resolved in the course of working on it (for instance, the inclusion of the Chorale, and the design of the beginning of the second part—originally planned as a Sonata movement—as a composed cadenza).

The following scheme[23] affords a general view of the total formal structure; the first three sections suggest an apotheosis of Berg's favourite form: symmetrical ternary form.[24]

Part I
    1. Andante (1-103)
After ten bars of introduction:
(11-37)—A
(38-83)—B un poco grazioso
(84-103)—A (abbreviated)
The end of A (28-37) forms the bridge to B; the same idea
reappears (77-83) in inversion, and in this form represents the
bridge into the reprise. In the middle section B notice the following correspondences: Cello (54-62=soloist (38-46): Horn
1 (63-70)=soloist (47-50); Trumpet 1 (70-74) plus Trombone
1 (74-76)=1st Violin (50-53) plus Viola (53). Soloist
(84-87)=(88-89)=(90-91)=Doublebass(11-14). The ending
takes up the introduction again; the last four bars (100-103)
are an ingenious transition to the following Allegretto: the 4/8
movement passes first into 3/8 and then into 6/8 movement.
    2. Allegretto (104-257)
(104-136)—A
(137-154)—B ('Quasi Trio I')
(155-166)—C ('Trio II')
(167-172)—B (abbreviated)
(173-257)—A
The main section A is a ternary form on its own: a1 (104-117),
a2 (118-126), and a1 (126-136). a1 combines three characteristics (Scherzando—Viennese—Rustico) which appear in a
different order at the repeat of a1. A Kärnten folk tune is
introduced in the last repeat of a1 *'come una pastorale'* (214) and
leads to the Coda which builds up to the stretto (240).

Part II
    1. Allegro (1-135)
(1-43)—A
(44-95)—B
(96-135)—A
A is distinctly binary: 'rubato' (1-22)—'molto ritmico' (23-
43). The 'main rhythm' (example 25) which dominates this

movement is introduced in bar 23. The 'liberamente' bar (43) is the first explicit mention of 'Es ist genug', as a monologue for the solo violin. The middle section B—a large solo episode—constitutes a ternary form on its own: (44–53) and (78–95) are based on the Trio II from part I. Elements of the Andante introduction and the Allegretto form the bridge to the reprise, which is an almost complete repeat of A, but with the order changed. The following bars (125–135)—representing a gradual collapse—make up the transition to the following.

2. Adagio (136–230)
(136–157)—Chorale
(158–177)—1st Variation
(178–197)—2nd Variation
(198–213)—Kärnten folk tune ('Molto Tranquillo')
(214–230)—Coda

In the first variation the Chorale melody appears in canon between cellos and harp (158–164); the trombone takes it over at bar 164. In the second variation it appears in inversion: horns (178–189), tuba and harp (185–190), trombones (190–198), cellos (198–199). The solo violin introduces the 'plaint' in bar 164 which culminates in the 'climax of the Adagio' (186). Coda: The Chorale in the orchestra (214–229), the opening of the Andante introduction 'as if in the distance' (229–230). The solo violin (215–230) resolves the plaint into the basic series.

Besides the symmetries in the large-scale construction demon-strated in the scheme above, there exist a rich host of references in all the subdivisions, starting with periodic formations in which the basic shape and its inversion correspond with each other like statement and answer, and finishing with mysterious relationships of numbers of bars as in the Chamber Concerto.

Even if all this is not directly perceptible to the listener, yet a part of the convincing effect that the Concerto produces in performance rests on the perfect equilibrium of the proportions.

The thematic layout is conditioned by two elements: by the twelve-note series which is the basis of the whole work (example 26) and by the Bach Chorale, the beginning of which

26

(example 27a) is identical with the last four notes of the series, while the end (example 27b) represents the inversion of the

27

series from the eighth to the eleventh notes. These correspondences alone provide numerous possible combinations, and they are exploited in the work.

The series itself was chosen by Berg so that it rests on the open strings of the violin (G D A E) like supporting pillars, in a way analogous to the use of the key of D major in the violin concertos of the classical period (in this key the open strings represent tonic, dominant and sub-dominant). The major, minor, diminished and augmented triads and seventh chords that are contained in the series and richly exploited in the Concerto can be read off from the basic series without any difficulty. Another important point is that the inversion of the first nine notes of the series is identical with its retrograde.

The appearance of the chord formations mentioned above should not be understood as representing an intention to establish a frame of reference based on particular fundamental tones —i.e. tonality in the earlier sense. The chords are used in the framework of the twelve-note structure determined by the series, and generally speaking they do not fulfil any cadential functions. The beginning of the stretto in the first part (240–241) may serve as an illustration of this principle of design (example 28): it is based on the inversion of the series begin-

ning on E-flat. Example 29 shows the beginning of the Allegretto, which is based on the series on D and A.

The bridge from the climax of the Allegro (II/125) into the Chorale melody may serve as a further example of the art of the 'smallest transition', a technique brought here to a pitch of inspired mastery. The nine-part chord in bar 125 contains the first nine notes of the series on C-sharp; the remaining three (G B A) are saved up for the unison in the next bar, in which the first note of the Chorale also appears in the solo violin. By bar 128 the soloist has already taken over two notes of the Chor-ale, and the chord is reduced to seven notes. By bar 130 the soloist has three notes of the Chorale and the chord is reduced to six notes. By bar 131 there are four notes in the solo part and only five in the chord. Finally in bar 134, over a pedal point on F, the full Chorale opens in the violas, followed canonically by the solo violin in bar 136.[25] The pedal point itself, as the dom-inant of the Chorale tonality B-flat major, prepares the way (from bar 111) for the Chorale's entry.

The particular skill in formal and thematic design, which very subtly creates the apparent technical 'simplicity'[26] of the work, corresponds to the composer's 'virtuosity' referred to by Berg in the dedicatory letter on the Chamber Concerto. But the soloist is also set specifically virtuoso tasks. The equivalent thematic treatment of soloist and orchestra in Part I meant that the main problem was the violinistic transmutation of the thematic content. The dialogue of Part II presents quite different problems: the techniques of harmonics and double-stopping are stretched to the utmost, and the execution of the 'plaint' and the matter of the direction of the whole body of violins and violas make enormous demands on the soloist's performing ability and expressive strength. Berg concerned himself with problems specific to the violin only while he was working on the Violin Concerto; it was very important to him to test the technical performability of each section with Krasner as soon as it was written. In every case it became apparent that the content that the composer wanted had been perfectly expressed in the violin part, and that all the technical difficulties in the solo part could be overcome by serious study.

The Violin Concerto was premièred at the ISCM Festival in Barcelona on 19th April 1936. Hermann Scherchen conducted, as Webern had declined the undertaking the previous day. There followed performances in London (Webern and Sir Henry Wood), Vienna (Otto Klemperer), Paris (Charles Münch), Boston and New York (Serge Koussevitsky). Louis Krasner was the soloist in each case.

Hearing it in the flesh brought out clearly the backward-glancing and summing-up features of the concerto. The relationship with Mahler's world is very clear in the dance characteristics of the work. As in most of Berg's works there are numerous quotation-like references to earlier tonal spheres, analogous to some passages in *Wozzeck*. The transparent instrumentation and clear demarcation of main voices and accompaniment are hallmarks of the Violin Concerto just as they are of the aria *Der Wein* and the opera *Lulu*. The concertante aspect represents a development of the Chamber Concerto, whose slow movement contains many germs that were to mature in the later work. The joining up of the separate sections finally is reminiscent of the unfolding of the Lyric Suite; the qualification of the work as 'latent drama' and some similarity of tone are further features that these two works have in common. The use of the Chorale, however, is a significant new element in Berg's creative development. As if in response to an appeal to a world existing before and above the tragic struggle, the Chorale intervenes in the drama with the power of some decisive judgment.

Part III   Three Articles by Berg

WHY IS SCHÖNBERG'S MUSIC SO DIFFICULT TO UNDERSTAND?

To answer this question one might be inclined to trace the ideas in Schönberg's work, to investigate his works from the point of view of thought. In other words, to do what is frequently done: get to grips with music by means of philosophical, literary or other arguments. That is not my intention! I am concerned solely with what happens musically in Schönberg's works; the compositional mode of expression which, like the language of any work of art (which we have to accept as a premise), must be considered the only one adequate to the object to be repre⁄sented. To understand this language through and through and grasp it in all its details, i.e. (to express it quite generally) to recognize the beginning, course and ending of all melodies, to hear the sounding⁄together of the voices not as a chance phenomenon but as harmonies and harmonic progressions, to trace smaller and larger relationships and contrasts as what they are—to put it briefly: to follow a piece of music as one follows the words of a poem in a language that one has mastered through and through means the same—for one who possesses the gift of thinking musically—as understanding the work itself. So the question at the top of this investigation appears answered if we manage to test Schönberg's mode of musical expression with regard to its comprehensibility, and then draw conclusions as to what extent it can be grasped.

I want to do this, knowing that a great deal is achieved if it is demonstrated in the details, on a single example, which is selected at random insofar as there are only a few passages in Schönberg's works that would not be equally suitable for such an investigation:

Even though these ten bars (they are the first bars of the First
String Quartet in D minor) are no longer considered impossible
or even difficult to understand, twenty years after they were composed, yet there is still this to say about them: If, at a first hearing, one wishes only to recognize the main voice and follow it
through to the end of these ten bars, to feel the whole as a single
melody, which is what it is and consequently ought to be just as
whistlable as the beginning of a Beethoven quartet—yes, even
if that is all the listener wishes to do, I am afraid he will find
himself faced with difficulties of comprehension as early as the
third bar. Accustomed to a melodic style whose most important property was symmetry of phrase construction, and adjusted
to a type of thematic construction that used only even-numbered
bar-relationships—a mode of construction that has dominated
all the music, with a few exceptions, of the last 150 years—an
ear so one-sidedly preconditioned will doubt the rightness of
the first bars of a melody that consists, contrary to all expectation,
of phrases of two and a half bars in length (example 30).

There is nothing new about thematic writing that avoids
two-bar and four-bar constructions. Just the opposite. Even
Bussler says quite rightly that 'it is just the greatest masters of
form (he means Mozart and Beethoven) who love free and bold
constructions and do not like to be confined within the gates
of even-numbered bar-relationships'. But really how seldom
such things occur in the classics (Schubert perhaps excepted),
and how such practice—so natural and easy in the eighteenth
century and earlier—has been lost in the music of Wagner and
the Romantics (apart from Brahms' folk song melody-types)
and therefore also in the whole new German School! Even
the *Heldenleben* theme which seemed so bold at the time is in
four- and two-bar phrases throughout, and after the usual

sixteen bars—the safest route to being understood—it comes back to a literal repeat of the first phrase. Even the music of Mahler and—to name a master of a quite different style— Debussy hardly ever deviates from melodic formations of an even numbers of bars. And if we consider Reger as the only one (besides Schönberg) who prefers fairly free constructions reminiscent of prose[27] (as he himself puts it) we have to admit that this is the reason why his music is relatively difficult of access. The *only* reason, I maintain. For neither the other pro- perties of his thematic writing (motivic development of multi- note phrases) nor his harmony—quite apart from his contra- puntal technique—are calculated to make his musical language difficult to understand.

With this state of affairs it is only too easy to see that a music which regards the asymmetrical and free construction of themes as just as available as the constructions with two-, four- and eight-bar phrases—and that is perhaps the most important aspects of Schönberg's way of writing—will not be easily understood, and in the case of his later works, not understood at all.

And when a theme like this (to come back to our particular case), in the course of the extremely fast development that is in keeping with its impetuous, even stormy character, right in the second repeat of that phrase that has hardly been grasped rhythmically—when this theme acquires the following ab- breviated form (example 31) by exercizing the right of varia- tion, the listener has lost the thread well before the first melodic

climax is reached two bars later (example 32). This semiquaver motif may well appear to fall from the clouds, whereas in fact

it is nothing other than the natural melodic continuation (again obtained by variation) of the main theme. This succession of chromatic side-steps actually presents an almost insuperable obstacle—as is clear in performances of the quartet even today —to the comprehension of the listener, who is accustomed to a slow development of themes or even a development obtained merely by sequences and unvaried repetitions. Generally he is not even able to relate these semiquaver figures to their chordal foundation (which is naturally there) on account of the speed of their succession; and he therefore loses his last possibility of orientation, of evaluating this passage at least on the basis of its cadential function, or of feeling it as a caesura or climax. No, it appears to him as a haphazard concatenation of 'caco-phonies' (caused by the zig-zagging—to him apparently sense-less—of the first violin); and then naturally he cannot make head or tail of the continuation, which presents new (though related) thematic formations and is already rich in motivic work, and leads back to a repeat of the main theme (in E-flat!) only after nineteen bars.

How much easier it would have been for the listener if all these things that are proving so difficult just did not exist; if the beginning of the quartet—may I be excused this impiety! —had had the following form, which purposely avoids such richness of rhythmic design, motivic variation and thematic work, and retains only the number of bars and notes of the unmurderable melodic inspiration (example 33):

33

This really removes the asymmetry of the original and provides a two-bar structure that will satisfy even the densest listener. The motivic and rhythmic development moves easily and slowly, evading every possibility of variation. Semiquavers, which might represent a stumbling block in the framework of an animated Alla Breve movement, are dispensed with entirely, and this removes the last impediment (namely the difficulty of hearing out those sequences of chromatic leaps of a seventh), since here too we do not overstep quaver movement, and even this is harmonized in half-bars. But in case this mangled theme should still be in danger of not being understood, the immediate and literal repetition in the tonic key offers a degree of general comprehensibility that verges on the popular, and to cap it all, all polyphony is avoided and the simplest imaginable accompaniment is put in its place.

What a difference when we look at Schönberg! 'The sketch-books he used while composing this String Quartet are of enormous importance for anyone interested in penetrating the psychology of his work. No one who has glanced at them will be able to say that Schönberg's music is constructed, intellectual or any other of the current catchwords with which people try to protect themselves from the superiority of his over-rich imagination.' For: 'Every thematic idea is invented together with all its counterpoints.'[28]

And it all has to be heard! At the beginning of the Quartet, in counterpoint with the first five-bar phrase of the first violin, there is an eloquent melody in the middle voice, built up—as an exception—of one- and two-bar phrases (example 34).

34

Even if this melody might escape one without damaging the general impression, it is inconceivable that anyone could grasp even the initial part of the main idea if they do not hear the expressive song of the bass line. And this can easily happen, since this melody is divided into two phrases, this time of *three* bars each (example 35). For this not to happen—if one does

not feel the beauty of such themes (and of this music in general) with the heart—it requires the hearing faculty at least of an external ear capable of keeping track of all the voices that are so pregnant in their different characters, and of recognizing as such the beginnings and endings (which are all at different points) of all these parts of melodies of different lengths, and of dwelling (with understanding) on their sounding together. And then, besides, it requires the hearing faculty of an ear that is set the most difficult task with regard to the rhythm, which —here and everywhere in Schönberg's music—rises to a hitherto unheard-of pitch of variety and differentiation.

Look at the cello part just quoted: how a skipping scale of dotted quavers has been developed[29] as early as the seventh bar out of the long-drawn legato phrases. Two bars later we hear in contrast the weighty crotchets of the seven-note theme storm-ing up in alternate fourths and thirds (E-flat, A-flat, C, F, A, D, F-sharp). Already two important motivic components of the Quartet have been exposed. And the way all these rhythmic forms are brought into contrapuntal relations with the other parts (which develop with quite different note-values and relationships)!

One would either have to be very deaf or very malicious to describe a music that manifests such richness of rhythms (and in such a concentrated form both successively and simul-taneously) as 'arhythmic'. If this word is intended to refer to all relations of tempo and note-values that are not directly derivable from mechanical movement (e.g. mill-wheel or railway train) or from bodily movement (e.g. marching, dancing, etc.) then by all means call Schönberg's music 'arhythmic'. But then the word must also be applied to the music of Mozart and all the classical masters except when they purposely aimed at uniform and therefore easily comprehensible rhythms, as in their dances and the movements derived from old dance forms (Scherzo, Rondo, etc.).

Or is 'arhythmic' intended as the opposite of some 'rhythm' that is no longer a musical concept, but a concept—like 'ethos', 'cosmos', 'dynamic', 'mentality' and other catchwords of our age—that can be applied 'in the last analysis' wherever there is something in motion, whether in art or in sport, philo-sophy or industry, world history or finance! A concept like this, which no longer stems from the mobile forms of music but is applied to something vague, something indefinable in musical terms, and which enables one to speak of the rhythm of a piece of music in the same way as one might speak of the rhythm of the recent slump—a concept like this is simply and naturally out of the question for anyone who can account for the rhythmic action—springing from the musical details—that extends over a whole work. The fact that such dilution of concepts can become current—even amongst those in whom one might least expect to find it (out of respect for their posi-tion): amongst some composers!—only proves how difficult it is for a music that wants to be measured only with the standards of its art (and not with the standards of some mere 'attitude'), —how difficult it is for such music to be understood.

And this brings us back to the real objective of my investiga-tion: the difficulty of understanding Schönberg's music. The difficulty arises from the music's richness—as we have seen so far—in beauties thematic, contrapuntal and rhythmic. It only remains to speak of the harmonic richness of this music, of the immeasurable cornucopia of chords and chordal connec-tions that are nothing other than the result of a polyphony (which we must also assess here) that is quite extraordinary in contemporary music. That is, they are the result of a juxtaposition of voices, distinguished by a hitherto unheard-of mobility in the melodic line. And so this excess of harmonic events is just as misunderstood as everything else. And naturally just as wrongly!

36

This passage (example 36) in Chorale style is not the chordal basis of the far-flung arches of an Adagio—which one could well imagine. No; it is merely the harmonic skeleton of the much-discussed beginning of this Quartet.

It seems incomprehensible that something so simple could be not understood—could even appear as an orgy of dissonances to a première audience hungry for sensation. And only the fact that such an unusual number and so many different kinds of chords are fitted into the narrow space of ten animated Alla Breve bars can explain why an ear—none too spoiled, on account of the relative poverty of other contemporary music—

is not equal to the task of digesting a sequence of fifty or more chords in a few seconds, and therefore presumes it 'hyper⁄trophied' (another of those sticks for belaying this music) where actually it is merely rich to overflowing. For, as the last example is supposed to show, the constitution of the chords and their respective combinations cannot be responsible for the difficulty experienced in understanding them. There is no single sonority, not even on the unaccented semiquavers of these ten quartet bars, that cannot be immediately clear to any ear educated in the harmony of the last century. Even the two whole⁄tone chords (marked with asterisks) with their chromatic preparations and resolutions—today nobody could pretend to be morally outraged by such things without be⁄coming the laughing stock of the whole musical world.

From this we can also see how irrelevant it is—and always was—to speak (in judging Schönberg's music) of how *regard⁄less* 'modern' voice⁄leading has become, and how it ignores the sonorities that result. What I have shown with regard to these ten bars can be demonstrated equally in every passage of this work. Even the boldest harmonic developments are far from being a playground of uncontrollable, coincidental sonorities. Chance has no place here, and anyone who still cannot follow may take the blame on himself, having full con⁄fidence in the ear of a master who can conceive all these things that appear so difficult to us with the same ease as he solves the most complicated counterpoint problems in front of his pupils' eyes as though he were conjuring the solution from up his sleeve. Asked once if 'he had ever properly heard' a passage in one of his works that was particularly difficult to understand, he answered with a joke that contains a profound truth: 'Yes, when I was composing it!'

A way of writing conditioned by such unwavering musi⁄cality contains all compositional possibilities, and therefore it can never be completely fathomed. Not even theoretically. The results of my analysis so far (and I would dearly like it to be complete) have by no means exhausted the possibilities of these few bars. For example, we still have to mention that these voices, invented from the start in the relationship of double counterpoint, permit of manifold variety also from the point of view of polyphonic technique, and this naturally comes to fruition in the various reprises of the main idea. First the melodies of violin and cello change places (since all mechanical repetitions are avoided even in this early work of Schönberg's). Presented graphically: the lines that appear in the first bars of the Quartet in the vertical position

1

2

3

are later introduced (page 5 of the miniature score) in the order

3 (in octaves)

2

1

At their third appearance (page 8) the subsidiary voices are already varied, though the melody notes are strictly preserved. Here the order is

2 (variant in semiquavers)

1 (in octave)

3 (decorated with quaver triplets)

Finally in the last reprise of the main idea (page 53) the main and subsidiary voices—quite apart from the innumerable com-binations with other themes in the work—appear in the fol-lowing order:

3 (variant in quaver triplets, but different from the preceding)

1 (in octaves)

[3   Inversion in quaver 'diminution']

But these first ten bars and their varied repeats represent a very, very small fraction of the work, which lasts about an hour. They can only give a hint of an idea of the harmonic, poly-phonic and contrapuntal occurrences (in an excess unheard-of since Bach) that flourish so luxuriantly in the thousands of bars of this music. One can assert this without being guilty of any exaggeration: Every smallest turn of phrase, even accompani⁄ mental figuration is significant for the melodic development of the four voices and their constantly changing rhythm—is, to put it in one word, thematic. And this within the framework of a single large symphonic movement whose colossal architec⁄ ture it is quite impossible to go into—even superficially—in the space of this investigation.

It is not surprising that an ear accustomed to the music of the last century cannot follow a piece of music where such things are going on. The music of the nineteenth century is almost always homophonic; its themes are built symmetrically in units of two or four bars; its evolutions and developments are for the most part unthinkable without an abundance of repetition and sequences (generally mechanical), and finally this conditions the relative simplicity of the harmonic and rhythmic action. Decades of habituation to these things make the listener of today incapable of understanding music of a different kind. He is irritated even by such things as a revival of some artistic technique that has become a rarity, or by deviations—even in only one of these musical matters—from what happens to be usual, even if these deviations are perfectly permissible from the point of view of the rules. Now imagine his position when (as in the music of Schönberg) we find— united, occurring simultaneously—all these properties that are otherwise considered the merits of good music, but which generally crop up only singly and well distributed amongst the various musical epochs.

Think of Bach's polyphony; of the structure of the themes— often quite free constructionally and rhythmically, of the classi⁄ cal and pre⁄classical composers, and of their highly skilled treatment of the principle of variation; of the Romantics, with their bold juxtapositions (which are still bold even today) of distantly related keys; of the new chordal formations in Wagner arrived at by chromatic alteration and enharmonic change, and their natural embodiment in tonality; and finally think of

Brahms' art of thematic and motivic work, often penetrating into the very smallest details.

It is clear that a music that unites in itself all these possibilities that the masters of the past have left behind would not only be *different* from a contemporary music where such a combination is not to be found (as I will show); it also—despite those properties that we recognized as the merits of good music, and despite its excessive richness in all the fields of music, or rather, just *because* of this—it also manages to be difficult to understand, which indeed Schönberg's music is.

I will be reproached with having proved something in this investigation where no proof was called for: namely the difficulty of the Quartet in D minor, a 'tonal' work that stopped being a problem long ago, a work in fact that has on the contrary been generally recognized and hence—understood! Well, even though the validity of that is questionable, I admit that the question at the head of this article would only really be answered if I were to demonstrate what I have shown on the basis of these few minor-key bars with reference to at least one example of so-called 'atonal' music. But it was not only a question of the difficulty but also—as readers of my analysis must have realized—a question of proving that the means of this music, despite the fact that much in it is felt to be particularly difficult to understand, are all right and proper: right and proper, naturally, in connection with the highest art! And it was of course easier to show this with regard to an example rooted in major/minor tonality, which nevertheless—an advantage in this connection—occasioned as much outrage in its day as 'atonal' music does today. But having arrived at a point where I regard the latter as just as 'existent' as the former (and it does exist, not only thanks to the work of Schönberg, 'the father of atonal thought' as he is generally called, but thanks also to the work of a large proportion of the musical world), all I need do is to project everything I said about these ten bars of the Quartet onto any passage in his later and most recent works.[30] Our title question is then equivalently answered by producing evidence that the means of this music are equally right and proper to the highest art. Indeed, it will then become apparent that the difficulty of understanding is not caused so much by the so-called 'atonality', which has meanwhile become the mode of expression of so many contemporaries, but here too by the other aspects of the structure of Schönberg's music, by the plenitude of artistic means applied here and everywhere in this harmonic style too, by the application of all the compositional possibilities provided by centuries of music, to put it briefly: by its immeasurable richness.

Here too we find the same multiplicity in the harmony, the same multi-level definition of the cadence;

here too the unsymmetrical and completely free construction of themes, together with their unflagging motivic work;

here too the art of variation, affecting both thematic work and harmonization, both counterpoint and rhythm of this music;

here too the same polyphony extending over the whole work, and the inimitable contrapuntal technique;

here too, finally, the diversity and differentiation of the rhythms, of which we can only say again that besides being subject to their own laws, they are subject also to the laws of variation, thematic development, counterpoint and polyphony. So in this field too, Schönberg attains to an art of construction that proves how wrong it is to speak of a 'dissolution of rhythm' in his music.

Considered from such a universal point of view, how basically different is the image of other contemporary composers, even those whose harmonic language has broken with the domination of the triad. The musical means listed above can naturally be demonstrated in their music too. But we never find them, as we do in Schönberg, united in the work of a single personality, but distributed amongst the various groups, schools, generations and nations and their respective representatives.

One composer may prefer a polyphonic style of writing, but

reduces this thematic development and the art of variation to a minimum. Another may write a bold harmonic style and not shrink from any combination of tones, but he has room only for melodies that hardly overstep homophony and are further characterized by the use of only two/ or four/bar phrases. One composer's 'atonality' consists in setting false basses under primitively harmonized periods; others write in two or more (major or minor) keys simultaneously, but the musical pro/ cedures within each one often betray a frightening poverty of invention. Music distinguished by its rich and animated melody and free construction of themes, sickens on the sluggish harmony, the symptoms being: poverty of intervallic move/ ment, long held chords, endless pedal points and harmonic progressions that perpetually recur. Music of this kind—I can almost positively assert this as a general proposition—cannot sur/ vive without more or less mechanical repetitions and, often, the most primitive sequential procedure. This is especially clear in the rhythm, bordering on monotony, in which a profusion of shifts and changes of metre conceals the neediness of the music. The rhythm—now rigid, how hammering, now dancing (and other kinds of animation)—provides more often than one would think the only handhold for a music that is otherwise com/ pletely inconsequential. And it is the representatives of this compositional technique who are generally referred to as 'strongly rhythmic composers'.

Even 'atonal' and otherwise 'progressively orientated' music manages to be accepted and even become relatively popular thanks to its adherence to such more or less established prin/ ciples, such exaggerated one/sidedness, and thanks to the fact that it contents itself with being 'modern, but not ultra'. And even if one or more aspects of such music do present the listener with difficult tasks, it adheres so strictly to the conven/ tional in all other respects—often being intentionally 'primi/ tive'—that it appeals to the ears of people of moderate musical discernment, just on account of those negative properties. It appeals to them all the more because the authors of such music,

in order to be stylistically pure, have to be aware of the consequences of only their one particular feature of modernity, and
are not compelled to draw conclusions from the combination
of all these possibilities.

The inescapable compulsion which consists (I repeat) in
drawing the farthest conclusions from a self-chosen musical
universality is to be found in one place only, and that is in
Schönberg's compositions. In saying this, I am, I believe, producing the last and perhaps the strongest reason for the difficulty
of understanding it. The circumstance that this noble compulsion is met by a sovereignty worthy of genius justifies me—
like everything that I have said about Schönberg's mastery,
unequalled by any of his contemporaries—in supposing—no,
it is no supposition, it is a certainty—that here we are dealing
with the work of one of the very few masters who will bear the
title 'classic' for time everlasting—long after the 'classicists of
our time' have become a thing of the past. Not only has he
'drawn the last and boldest conclusions from German musical
culture' (as Adolf Weissmann aptly says in his book *Die
Musik in der Weltkrise*), he has got further than those who seek
new paths blindly and—consciously or unconsciously—more
or less negate the art of this musical culture. So today on
Schönberg's fiftieth birthday one can say, without having to be
a prophet, that the work that he has presented so far to the world
ensures not only the predominance of his personal art, but what
is more that of German music for the next fifty years.

ALBAN BERG

*From the special number of 'Musikblätter des Anbruch' to celebrate Schön-
berg's fiftieth birthday, 13th September 1924*

THE MUSICAL IMPOTENCE OF
HANS PFITZNER'S 'NEW AESTHETIC'

'But with a melody like that one is suspended in mid-air. One can only recognize its quality, not demonstrate it; there is no agreement to be reached about this quality by intellectual means: either one understands it by the rapture it arouses, or one does not. Whoever cannot go along with it cannot be converted by any arguments, and there is nothing to say against someone who attacks it except to play the melody and say "how beautiful". What the melody says is as deep and as clear, as mystical and as obvious as the Truth.'[31]

It may be a severe disappointment for many musicians—as it is for me—to see such words written by a composer of Pfitzner's standing. And that in a book bursting with erudition, that hardly leaves a single sphere of human knowledge untouched and shows itself as it were orientated in philosophy and politics, history of music and race theory, aesthetics and morality, journalism and literature, and God knows what else.

But in the field where knowledge would be most imperative, in the field of things musical, it is simply denied us, and the writer assumes a point of view which precludes from the start any possibility of distinguishing good from bad. And then he continues (in highly ungrammatical German):

'So I speak the following only to a small group, namely those who still have and want to have a sense of the quality of a melody—a sense that has been driven out of us with strongly increasing success since decades ago.'

But he does not say a single word to this small group—amongst which I presume to count myself—which could be of assistance to that 'sense' or even takes account of it. Instead he issues the equally German exhortation (German in sentiment this time rather than in the mode of expression):

'So we who still have this sense, let us courageously enthuse!'

For my part I would rather leave the enthusing to that large group who do not need to have the 'sense of the quality of a melody' 'driven out' of them (because they don't have it), and reserve for myself and the few others who managed to escape (all the enthusing) a worthier, and in any case more matter-of-fact relationship to music. But it turns out on the other hand that the small group that Pfitzner calls on is not so small after all, for he feels able to present their musical sense with the following indescribably difficult and even problematic case:

No. 7 of Schumann's *Kinderszenen: Träumerei*. Not one of the many hundreds of melodies—that are not so generally familiar—from classical symphonic music or chamber music, but the very composition that even in Schumann's day enjoyed a great and uncontested success, and one which since then, as far as I know, has not been subjected to any particularly sharp 'attack'.

So the praise that Pfitzner lavishes on the *Kinderszenen* seems all the more unnecessary, and does not testify to any particular 'courage':

'Each of the little pieces in this opus is a musical shape of fine charm, poetry and musicality, and above all highly personal in character.'

And when he goes on:

'But could anyone who understands the primeval language of music fail to recognize that *Träumerei* is quite uniquely distinguished by the quality of the melody?'

that is applicable only in so far as this piece is 'quite uniquely distinguished' in another way, so uniquely that Pfitzner describes it on the very next page as 'not really belonging in the *Kinderszenen*'.

But I assert (besides what I have to say later about the quality of this melody) that *Träumerei* is already distinguished by its

central position as No. 7 of thirteen pieces, and occupies therefore a very special position in the symmetrical structure of the
whole opus, and is a vital component—perhaps the most vital
—of the whole. This can only be overlooked when as a matter
of principle one turns one's back on any 'agreement by intellectual means'. If one does not do that, and allows the 'sense
for the quality of a melody' (doubtless including a sense of its
tonality) to function for once instead of letting it be confiscated
by a small group, then it will certainly strike one that *Träumerei*
is also distinguished from the point of view of tonality. It is
the first of the *Kinderszenen* in a flat key and shares this property
with only the following piece *Am Kamin* (which is also related
to it in other ways).

But Pfitzner prefers to close his eyes to all that. Rather he is
concerned in general, and also in the special case of *Träumerei*,
with nothing less than the 'primeval language of music' and:

'For whoever does not understand it, *Träumerei* is a little
piece in song-form with the tonic, dominant, sub-dominant,
and other closely related keys—without deviation from the
normal, as far as the elements are concerned; no harmonic
novelty, no rhythmic finesse, the melody rising through the
notes of the triad, "for piano, two hands".'

Not the layman—who confronts this composition with per-
plexity—but the musically educated (who possesses the faculty
of recognizing it theoretically) is told once and for all that his
education is of no use to him if he does not understand the
primeval language of music. And if he does understand this
language his theoretical faculties are not at all necessary, since
'with a melody like this' one is 'suspended in mid-air' anyway.

'A melody like this', we may mention in passing, means 'a
beautiful, truly genial melody', 'a genuine musical inspiration',
without any other evidence being brought forward, whether
for its beauty, its genius, or its genuineness, except that 'the
desire to explain it is a dilettante undertaking'. For:

'When we are faced with something ungraspable that defies
our explanation, we are happy to loosen the strict succession of

thoughts, surrender the weapons of reason and declare ourselves completely captive, dissolving defencelessly in feeling. To
a genuine musical inspiration all one can really say is "How
beautiful it is!". Anything closer, any word in the direction of
"Why?" belittles the impression received, injures the spiritual
phenomenon, destroys the "breath" of the "poem".'[32]

Pfitzner manages, even in the case under discussion, to avoid
these three dangers simply by regarding all purely musical
arguments as dealt with in these few theoretical morsels quoted
earlier.

His next cry—'But for us who know, what a miracle of
inspiration!'—arouses the pleasant hope that we will after all
hear something musically revealing about *Träumerei* from someone who understands the melody and the primeval language of
music in general, that is, from 'someone who knows' and not
from some 'enthusiast' who merely surrenders himself to his
'feelings'. But we are fobbed off with a question that even
manages to elude any sort of knowledge:

'What can be said about it that will make it accessible to the
understanding of one who does not feel this melody "through
and through", this melody which is at the same time the whole
piece, and where form and idea are practically identical?
Nothing.'

Admitted! But there ought to be something one can say
about the quality of the melody to someone who *does* feel it
through and through. Even if only about a negative example—
any old piece of *kitsch*—which does not have to be felt through
and through! For if it really was impossible to produce any
'arguments' except those of feeling then anyone would have the
same right to 'enthuse into the illimitable' in the same tone as
Pfitzner about any inspiration which he feels to be 'beautiful',
'genial' and 'genuine', and one would not be able to contradict
him. If one reads these quotations from Pfitzner substituting
Hildach for Schumann (for example) and *Lenz* for *Träumerei*,
anyone who does not contest the right to 'dissolve defencelessly
in feeling' would have to 'surrender the weapons of reason'

and 'declare himself completely captive' to such a courageous Hildach-enthusiast.

That cannot be! There must be some possibility of saying something irrefutable about the beauty of a melody, something that will 'make it accessible to the understanding' and awaken a sense of its quality. Naturally something of a musical nature; not purely matters of feeling and all too personal enthusiasm that cannot be implemented by any evidence, such as the following:

'I can speak of the nobility of the language of sound, of the absolute originality, deeply personal quality and pristine peculiarity of the melody, of its German-ness, delicacy, inti-macy—it is as though the words were flitting round in circles in front of the notes'—it certainly is—'all of them together can-not come close to saying what it is that makes the melody what it is.'

And that is right too! Nevertheless he does attempt to get to grips with the beauty of this piece by calling it (after he has established that it is a *Träumerei* and not for heaven's sake 'anything in the nature of a "rêverie" '):

'thoughtful, serious feeling, deeply losing itself, fine-souled and yet powerful. The well-known head of Schumann with his head supported on his hand can give an idea of this. One can enthuse on into the illimitable in this way without managing to conjure up the magic of this music in words. It is a drop of music from the deepest spring; we too (?) are musically de-praved and lost if we dissociate ourselves from this beauty.'

Yes, but we are also musically depraved and lost if we can find—and consider possible—no explanation (that brings us closer to the art) of this beauty except comparisons borrowed from all fields (but not music) and springing from a mood more tipsy than 'fine-souled'.[33]

It could be objected that the writings of the old masters sometimes contain descriptions of the sort that I am taking exception to, and that my criticism therefore applies not only to Pfitzner but also to Schopenhauer, Wagner or Schumann (for example). My reply to this—without involving myself in the pros and cons of such musical description and the extent to which they are acceptable today—is that this sort of enthusiastic musical description only had sense when the world's attention had to be drawn to the beauty of a particular work, when this beauty had to be revealed. And this usually required more courage than sticking up for *Träumerei*, which—as I mentioned before—charmed and impressed the whole musical world from the first day it appeared. And remember that such literary remarks were always accompanied—when they originated from a significant composer (think of Schumann's *Writings on Music and Musicians*)—by purely musical discussion, usually on a very high level. And when this was so, an exhaustive and relevant analysis was usually provided as well.

In Pfitzner's book—which pretends to so much erudition in other respects—we are denied the very erudition which could convince us of his opinions. And wherever he does use his erudition and theorizes, he does it in such a nonchalant and insufficient—even false—manner that (I must repeat what I said at the beginning) the unenlightened reader imagines he has in front of him a book by a philosopher or politician or other kind of scholar writing a *Feuilleton*, but never by a composer of Pfitzner's standing.

For how can such a composer dismiss the melody of *Träumerei* with the words 'rising through the notes of the triad'? The beauty of this melody does not actually lie so much in the large number of motivic ideas, but in the three other characteristic features of beautiful melodies. Namely: the exceptional preg-nancy of the individual motifs; their profuse relations with one another; and the manifold application of the given motivic material (see example 37).

The fact that the melody 'rises through the notes of the triad' is its least recommendation. My feeling is—to take only this recurrent rising phrase (see the motif marked *a*)—that the auxiliary note E, dissonant with respect to the F major triad disposed as a succession of notes, is the characteristic and

charming element. And we must not forget that this whole turn of phrase is felt immediately as a variation (and what a variation!) of the initial leap of a fourth. This leap also survives in the motif of the descending phrase (b, c, d) constantly changing into different intervals (m) by taking advantage of every opportunity provided by the harmony.

For reasons of space I can only hint at the other melodic variants. Notice particularly the variants of the above-mentioned descending phrase (x, y, z). I cannot pass over the last appear⁄ance of this phrase (z) without remarking that there is hardly anything one could say about it that would be less characteristic than Pfitzner's phrase about 'feeling deeply losing itself.'[34] From the highest note of this little four⁄bar sentence we descend over a sixth for the first time, and this by means of a motivic 'inversion' made up of interval steps, and, for the first time, an intervallic leap. It is this inversion which Pfitzner's phrase so utterly fails to describe, this melodic return home, which is a return to the starting point from the harmonic point of view as well.

Pfitzner's verdict on the rhythm of this melody is equally irrelevant. He cannot find any 'finesse' in it, although the shift of accent between strong and weak parts of the bar persists throughout the whole piece and must strike any musical listener as just such 'finesse'. This shift is evident in the first two bars, produced by the rising figure *a* which shifts the up⁄beat rhythm to a position one crotchet further on. It is still more evident when one observes the half⁄closes and full closes of the individual little four⁄bar sentences from this point of view. These end as follows:

at A (and E) on the second crotchet
at B (after a grace⁄note) on the third crotchet
at C on the fourth quaver

The next sentence, which is apparently a sequential repeat of the preceding, does not close on the third crotchet (which would have been perfectly admissible harmonically) but— extending beyond it—

at D on the fourth crotchet.

Finally the last bar brings a close that is certainly different rhythmically from that of the second sentence:

at F on the third crotchet.

After what I have said so far, it will have to be admitted that by describing and 'demonstrating' in this way we obtain a different, a more closely approximative image of the 'quality of a melody' than Pfitzner was capable of giving with his enthusing words and his insufficient analysis which falsified the musical facts. In the music example I have tried to show (quite casually, in the first four bars notated above Schumann's original) how poverty-stricken such a melody looks when it does not possess, for example, the melodic refinements that I have listed, and of which one could really say merely that it 'rises through the notes of the triad' and lacks 'rhythmic finesse'. I have retained a second motif (the descending one, which Pfitzner does not even consider worth the trouble of men-tioning) at least in the needy form *s*, and I have not changed Schumann's (by no means ordinary) harmonic skeleton.

But Pfitzner rides rough-shod over the harmony too. He refers to the 'tonic, dominant, and sub-dominant', but pretends to know nothing of any 'deviation from the usual, as far as the elements are concerned'. And yet what individuality we find here too! Both as regards the structure within the individual sentences (notice, for example, in the first four-bar sentence how the changes of harmony proceed in the following increasing and decreasing note-values: 5/4, 3/4, 1/4, 2/4, 1/8, 1/8, 1/4, 3/4 and then back to 5/4, etc.) and as regards the disposition with reference to the whole piece and its prominent points. These points—I am referring to the separate melodic climaxes of each of the six sentences—occur on the following chords, which get stronger harmonically in the order of their appear-ance:

at G (and K) on a triad
at H on a seventh chord
at I (and J) on a ninth chord with minor ninth.

The second repeat of the first eight bars should bring (if we were really dealing with a 'little piece in song-form with tonic, dominant and sub-dominant') a mechanical repetition of the harmonic events of the first eight bars (G and H), with the second four-bar sentence providing the final return to the tonic (e.g. by transposition a fourth higher). But how is the tonic reached in actuality! Instead of the expected seventh chord (belonging to the region of the sub-dominant) of the corres- ponding point H, we now hear at the last climax:

at L a ninth chord, this time with a major ninth.

The strongest chord harmonically has been saved up for the end, and the cadence which follows it can truly be said to represent a 'deviation from the usual': it contains one and the same cadential motif (c2) twice in succession (the only time in the whole piece that this happens), harmonized in two different ways. And although it goes without saying that the conception of this piece—and composition in general—takes place in a sphere far removed from theoretical deliberations, yet it would hardly be possible to design an ending like this with- out artistic intention and the conscious exercise of technical musical ability.

We are all the more justified, even compelled (if we wish to form a judgment about music) to give an account of this from a musico-theoretical point of view as well, and further make it as precise and foolproof as possible. But not like Pfitzner, whose manner of making musical 'personal descrip- tions' is reminiscent of the conventional 'official descriptions' where everything is represented as being 'usual' and 'normal'. Some ossifying official would have no scruples about writing the usual 'special distinguishing marks: None' even under the picture of Schumann's head supported on his hand.

Pfitzner does exactly the same with *Träumerei!* He even goes further: he makes the composition seem quite insignificant, normal and lacking in distinguishing marks by representing it as a sort of bagatelle 'for piano two hands' (even putting the phrase in inverted commas). Well, a brief glance at the music is enough to convince anyone that this is a strict piece of four- part writing (with the exception of a couple of points) which, as far as the style, character, contrapuntal technique, range of the individual parts and their playability and singability are concerned, could easily be given to a string quartet or wind ensemble, or even to the four singing voices.

There is a great difference between this composition (notice for example the four-part imitation at *e*)—even though it appeared as a piano piece and is only valid as such—and the sort of composition that is dismissed as 'for piano two hands', a genre that is basically restricted to a homophonic style in which melody and accompaniment are each allotted one of the two hands. And it is a fact that the other pieces in the *Kinderszenen* do not possess this universal musical style, but use a pianistic style that takes into account—in a more or less artistic manner —the technique of the instrument.

This difference jumps to the eye when one turns to the piece following *Träumerei*: No. 8 *Am Kamin* (see the music example!). But the other pieces are 'piano pieces' even more than *Am Kamin*; for example No. 10 *Fast zu Ernst*. Of this whole series of character pieces this is the one that cannot be credited with any more significant distinction (nor any less significant distinction) than 'for piano two hands', whereas to describe *Träumerei* in this way is not only irrelevant but also—when it is stated so tendentiously—represents a disparagement of the style of this piece.

Such a disparaging tone with reference to the purely musical properties of this melody is supposed to create an impression of complete artlessness, despite which an effect as elevated as it is 'ungraspable' is obtained. And once this impression is created—with six lines of analysis in telegraphic style and five times as many lines of courageous enthusing—it is easy to draw the conclusion—and this is the direction that Pfitzner's writing intends to take—namely, that it is just as useless for modern music to surround itself with the odium of technical artistry and find 'theoretical support' for its horrors, as it is to try to find theoretical explanations for the beauty of classical music. Which is the reason why in the whole book there is not a single attempt with regard to an example taken from modern music to find a purely musical orientation for himself and his readers

about these horrors, and throw some light on them. The statements (printed with wide spacing) that 'musical impotence is
declared permanent and supported theoretically' and that 'music
no longer needs to be beautiful, and the composer need have no
ideas of his own' are considered sufficient. None of this can be
proved theoretically, any more than the opposite can be proved
with regard to classical music. A 'real, honest public' does not
need such art, and whoever pretends to feel the need for it is one of
those 'culture snobs or worse' who, as is well known, 'gobble up
everything like dogs: Beethoven today, Kandinsky tomorrow'.

Which is apparently conclusive evidence that 'a symptom of
decay' exists—a fact that was still called in question on the
title page.

It should now be my task, my duty even, to do what
Pfitzner has carefully neglected to do in his whole book.
Namely to speak of that modern music which he attacks from
literary, political and other points of view (but not from the
musical point of view) in a matter-of-fact way for once, and
demonstrate on at least one example how things stand today
with regard to those matters that go into the making of good
music: melodies, richness of harmony, polyphony, perfection
of form, architecture, etc. And if I succeeded in this as well as
I did with *Träumerei* I would have proved the existence of that
purely musical potency which Pfitzner fails to demonstrate
even in the cases of Beethoven, Schumann and Wagner, although his whole discussion of classical music was motivated
solely by the intention of exposing the music of today as
'impotent', and therewith striking it dead.

For my aim of rehabilitating modern music I would choose
—following a momentary impulse rather than with the intention of selecting particularly typical cases—two song-like
melodies (just as Pfitzner did): *Ach Knabe, du musst nicht
traurig sein!* from *Der Schildwache Nachtlied* by Mahler, and the
subsidiary theme of Schönberg's Chamber Symphony.

But this article is limited by considerations of space and I
cannot go into these examples here. Another time! But I may

be believed when I say that my proof of musical potency will
be successful. Perhaps my musico-theoretical remarks about
Schumann's *Träumerei* will be sufficient for that 'small group'
—apostrophized by me too—'who still have and want to have
a sense for melody'; at least they can serve as a suggestion as to
how modern melodies may be judged. Such things are not
simple! It might be more obvious and easier for that small group
to try using the negative procedure: namely, to take the standards that I applied to Schumann's *Träumerei* and am accustomed to apply in other cases, and apply them to a melody
which would frustrate my other trusted 'arguments' and 'explanations' if I wanted to bring theoretical proof of its beauty.

I choose—this time rather with the intention of selecting a
particularly typical case than following a momentary impulse
—a song composed in 1916 (so it is certainly modern) [From
Five Songs, Opus 26, by Hans Pfitzner]. Unfortunately I cannot reproduce it in full, and can only give a harmonic indication of the accompaniment ('rising through the notes of the
triad, for piano two hands') (example 38).

However, regard this melody with the same loving exactitude
—penetrating into all the musical aspects—that I devoted to
Träumerei, and you will not hold it against me if in this case I
make an exception and save myself the trouble of making a
penetrating musical analysis which would in any case only
'diminish the impression and injure the spiritual phenomenon'.
For truly:

With a melody like this one is suspended in mid-air. One
can only recognize its quality, not demonstrate it; there is no

agreement to be reached about this quality by intellectual means: either one understands it by the rapture it arouses, or one does not. Whoever cannot go along with it cannot be converted by any arguments, and there is nothing to say against someone who attacks it except to play the melody and say 'How beautiful!'. Which I do herewith.

ALBAN BERG

From 'Musikblätter des Anbruch', Vienna, second year, No. 11–12, June, 1920

TWO FEUILLETONS

A CONTRIBUTION TO THE TOPIC 'SCHÖNBERG AND MUSIC CRITICISM'

Much has been written about the inadequacy of the usual musical reports that appear in newspapers today. But nobody —to my knowledge—has written about the levity with which musical matters *in general* are dealt with. Both regrettable. For it is all too understandable and even, although distasteful, excusable that a criticism that wants to be more than a mere report (perhaps criticism should not try to be more than that) —should miss the point when the subject is, for example, a modern work. But that levity which spreads itself immediately whenever musical matters are touched on is reprehensible and inexcusable, since it sneers at any notion of the sacredness of Art. It can of course be accounted for, both by the general public's lack of musical culture—which is to the critic's advantage just as his own ignorance does not harm him (N.B. I am speaking of purely musical knowledge and not of musicohistorical knowledge)—and by the newspaper reader's good faith and respect in accepting everything that is put before him in the columns of his newspaper. This is particularly true with regard to matters where he does not feel so at home (as a consequence, as I said, of his lack of musical culture) as he does in the political and financial sections. A resourceful coverage also takes care to extenuate and even justify its facile *métier* by means of the occasional cleverly placed article. For instance, we are told in the 'Kleinen Chronik' of the *Neue Freie Presse*[35] on the occasion of the sixtieth birthday of the Berlin music critic Dr Leopold Schmidt that his reviews are 'founded on sound specialized knowledge and distinguished by his gift of judgment—a gift which is inborn like any other' and that 'this critical talent is supplemented by conscientiousness and a feeling of responsibility—qualities which as it were make up the character of the critic' and further that 'his presentation is soberly and straightforwardly matter-of-fact, and he clothes his judgment in a temperate form, which is an expression of that inner culture which is conscious of the wide range of critical words written in the pages of a great newspaper'. So it is not surprising that the newspaper reader, who is somewhat gullible anyway, is taken in by all the rest.

The following remarks, occasioned by two newspaper articles that I happened to read almost by chance (they probably repre-sent only a fraction of the music-critical outpourings of the past summer), may shed some light on how things really stand with regard to the 'sound specialized knowledge', the 'conscien-tiousness' and the 'feeling of responsibility', the 'sober, straight-forward matter-of-factness' and the 'temperate form which is an expression of that inner culture which is conscious of the wide range of critical words written in the pages of a great newspaper'.

One of them[36] contains, in the middle of a typical eight-column jumble of casual reviews juxtaposed with a forcible disregard of context, a reckoning with so-called 'atonal' music (there is not even a sub-heading to say that this subject is up for discussion). A problem like this, which is a subject of intense preoccupation for all thinking musicians today, the best of whom are perhaps on the way towards finding a solu-tion, is finally dealt with in *two* columns as a sort of appendage to the 'gleanings of the Vienna Music Festival'; and there is still enough space to prostrate once more—for the time being—the 'master of the atonal faith' Arnold Schönberg. All done in that 'temperate form in which . . . inner culture . . . wide range . . . great newspaper . . . etc. etc.'

And we read in the same *Feuilleton* that other music, truly insignificant music, is 'sure-footed, handled with spirit and animation, and sounds well *without distortion*' and 'should therefore be more highly prized today than in the more productive and *healthier* ages of music' and further 'that it did not *despise* the necessities of *ordered* musical language'. The intelligent reader knows already that the gibes I have italicized can only be intended for Schönberg. And whereas such works as these are appraised in this way, as soon as Schönberg's music and the '*great triumph*' of his direction, of 'atonal thought', comes under discussion, all they can talk about is a '*method*' whose 'only attraction lies in *provocation*',[37] and of '*contrived* intervals and sounds', of '*wilfully constructed* chords', of '*atrophied musical procreative power*', of '*melodies brewed in the test tube*', etc.

If critical words like these testify to 'sober, straightforward matter-of-factness', just wait until the critic brings his 'sound specialized knowledge' to bear on more *detailed* musical matters! The joke ends here! The joke that the reviewer can allow himself at the expense of his unwitting public, and which even I can enjoy in a *Feuilleton* in the *Neue Freie Presse*: *Where is it written, where is it implied, which of Schonberg's melodies for example could provide grounds for the statement* that 'our anarchists regard the laws of melody as slavery'? Further, that they are 'slaves of the chord'? *Let them show me any work of Schonberg's where such slavery is apparent, more apparent than it is in the work of the classical period.*

But our *Feuilleton* is not concerned with the *rightness* of the judgment. The newspaper reader is so fascinated by the image of anarchists being slaves at the same time, that he swallows everything else without wasting a moment's thought on it. The same applies to the assertion, dropped soon afterwards merely in passing, that the chords of these 'anarchists' are 'wilfully *deviating more and more from nature*'. The reader has of course no idea that this too is one of those problems that are best passed over with a *manner of speaking* that wilfully deviates more and more from the truth.

So it is all the more pleasant for the critic of this music, having got round everything problematical in this way, to dwell on the music's 'soul', which is obviously lacking, since 'so far at least' 'it has not been able to divulge itself' (namely to the music reviewer of this world newspaper), for which one cannot really blame it. Besides this lack, the other 'defects that are revealed drastically enough' are exposed by means of the following statements:

'Where is there a—"large-scale atonal form" is an expression we do not dare use—large-scale atonal outpouring? Atonality cannot produce any broader musical action within which fates and developments can be consummated, because nothing is coined, nothing *can* be coined that is capable of submitting to a fate or developing itself, for instance, a theme or some basic melodic idea. There is good reason why the master of the atonal faith has reached the aphoristic phase.'

Does it not make one clutch one's head when one reads revelations like this that so falsify the facts? Should not Herr Julius Korngold acquaint himself with the fact that Schönberg has written other works besides the Six Little Piano Pieces in the so-called 'atonal faith' —and the word 'aphorism' is anyway just as inapplicable to these pieces as to Schumann's short piano pieces, or Chopin's, or Beethoven's Bagatelles. Cycles of fifteen songs and twenty-one melodramas, and Schönberg's two stage works surely provide manifold evidence for the existence of 'larger atonal forms', and it is also possible to find—I am thinking now of the final part of *Erwartung* which is terrific both in range and in expression— what Korngold calls a 'larger atonal outpouring'.

And how does he visualize the design of the 'Jakobsleiter', an oratorio, that is, a form well known to provide occasion for 'broader musical action'? Might that not also provide occasion for the formation of 'themes' and 'basic musical ideas' that 'develop themselves' and 'undergo fates'?

Does he mean to tell us that he does not know anything about all that? Or does he think that these works in the larger forms really do not exist, because he keeps his mouth shut about them and pretends to know only aphorisms? And does he expect his readers at least to think likewise?

Never mind how these questions might be answered; the mere fact that anyone—be he the last reader of the *Neue Freie Presse*—is justified in posing them proves what the true situation is with regard to 'what goes to make up the character of the critic *as it were* (my italics): conscientiousness and a feeling of responsibility'. Impolite as we 'honoured disciples around Schönberg'[38] are, I will not allow ladies first even when con⁄ cerning myself with music reviewers of both sexes. I could not bring myself—even at the risk of just such another reproach— to sacrifice the artistic device of contrast (which would not have been so clear if the order had been different) to the social con⁄ veyance of politeness, which we usually 'hasten to observe' when we are 'making use of the great organs of public opinion'.

But I do not want to speak of that *Feuilleton* in which Dr Elsa Bienenfeld deals with us in this way (although one can draw the right conclusions about the methods and behaviour of Viennese newspaper criticism from *every* line she writes in the 'Neues Wiener Journal'). I want to speak of a more matter⁄of⁄ fact article entitled 'Against Modern Music'.[39] I am taking the artistic liberty of describing the article—which does not actually appear as a '*Feuilleton*', since there simply was no room for it in the Sunday cornucopia of belletristic outpourings in the 'Neues Wiener Journal' and it therefore had to be placed among the 'daily news items' (just like the diaries of Bahr and Wein⁄ gartner which were intended more for eternity than for the day on which they appeared)—anyway I take the liberty of des⁄ cribing this article as a '*Feuilleton*' since this is what it is in all but name. This liberty will possibly be held against me as another piece of bad manners, and not unjustly, after what I have been saying about musical *Feuilletons* in general.

Dr Bienenfeld's article deals with a recent abusive pamphlet by a certain Walter Krug, and deals with it in such a way that even the most resourceful reader, familiar with her style, can⁄ not with the best will in the world decide how much is mere *reporting* about the contents of the pamphlet, and how much is *her own judgment* about the things discussed in the pamphlet; there is no way of telling where the one stops and the other begins. The aim of these tactics is to deal a blow to Arnold Schönberg—who is torn to pieces anyway in the pamphlet—

off her own bat and in her own field of action. This goes so far —and one has to admit, with admiration, that her tactic achieves its end, despite the naivety with which it is done—that quotations from the pamphlet under review are either not pre/ sented as quotations or mutilated, as for example:

WALTER KRUG

(page 59) Everything that is held to live *below consciousness* as if in a dream, could be heard consciously in a favourable hour. And that be music. Such music is held to have an enor/ mous, flowing strength, and builds *according to none of the laws that we know.* It has a rhythm, just as the blood beats out its rhythm, and just as all life in us is held to be rhythm. It has a tonality, but as sea and storm have a tonality. It is held to have harmonies, but such harmonies as we *could not* grasp. We would never find its themes. There would *always* be a structure there, but we *could not* build an image of this structure in ourselves. All craft and technique is held to have perished in us, everything be united and one with the content. Everything that came under Music and Tradition had to fall. *This* is held to be the fulfilment of what we are afraid of; our unconscious twitchings are held to be represented; our fear of ghosts . . .

(page 66) . . . Suppose one *had imagined* that . . . etc.

. . . a sort of embryo or homunculus. *Or to put it differently:* since *musical language* and *harmony* are, according to the new theory's decree, against any agreement, *one has the impression as if someone wanted to invent new words* . . . etc.

DR ELSA BIENENFELD

(without quotation marks) Every/ thing that *lives in* consciousness as if in a dream could be heard in a favour/ able hour. And that be music. Such music is held to have an enormously flowing strength, and builds *according to laws that we do not know.*

It has a tonality, but as sea and storm have a tonality. It is held to have harmonies, but we *cannot* grasp them.

There would *now* be a structure there, but we *cannot* construct an image of it in ourselves.

Everything that came under Music and Tradition had to fall. *Such sounds* are held to be the fulfilment of what we are afraid of ; our unconscious twitch/ ings are held to be represented; our fear of ghosts . . . *Krug expresses his opinion in an equation:* 'Suppose one were to imagine that . . . etc.'

. . . a sort of embryo or homunculus. 'Or to put it differently: Since *harmony* and *musical language*, as decreed by *Schönberg's* new theory, are against any agreement, *they are as completely in/ comprehensible as if a writer, instead of . . .*' etc. . . . (and from here on quite differ/ ently and without any reference to the original text under discussion).

Or, such quotations are falsified by being placed in a wrong context:

'Krug's sharpest criticism is directed against Schönberg. One must really have very limited means if one decides to subsist on the whole-tone scale for the rest of one's musical life.'

It would never occur even to the writer of that virulent pamphlet to say anything quite so stupid about Schönberg. Still less to anyone who has any idea about modern music or is connected with it professionally. In reality the quoted words refer to *Debussy*, not Schönberg, where they at least have a sense from the harmonic point of view, although the spiteful conclusion is completely unjustified.

But Dr Elsa Bienenfeld's review—after succumbing to the temptation to reinforce the falsification with a 'That is certainly right!'—proceeds as follows, on her own account and at her own risk:

'But one must not underestimate the fact that the tools of harmony have certainly been made more wieldy by Schönberg's work. His first works are rich in melodic ideas, ingenious in form, and masterly in everything to do with polyphony.'

And—assuming this—*she now succeeds in writing a sentence, which*—with reference to the rightness of the ideas that it is sup-posed to express, to the exactitude of the quotation it contains, to the temperamental tone in which it is couched, to the lapidary simplicity with which the several trains of thought are combined with one another, and even with reference to the punctuation which makes such combination possible—*may not be coined again in the near future and can surely have no parallel even in contemporary music criticism*:

'But Schönberg renounces all this in his later experiments, *Art* (Kunst) *does not come from "to come"* (Kommen), *but from "to be able"* (Können), *as he is fond of saying.*'

How differently, in how much more temperate a form, with what sound, straightforward matter-of-factness—to put it briefly: with how much more inner culture would Korngold have let us know that Schönberg's later compositions are not compositions at all, but '*experiments*' in which this '*anarchist*' *even* '*renounces*' his 'melodic ideas', 'ingenious form' and 'everything to do with polyphony', which is not surprising from one who now only composes 'aphorisms' according to a 'method', and is a 'slave of the chord' besides. And how different that quotation from Schönberg would have looked if Korngold had quoted it. A man who could not even claim to have heard what 'Schönberg is *fond* of saying' but can at best have read in Schönberg's article *Problems of Art Instruction*[40] that Art probably 'does not come from ability (*Können*=to be able) but from necessity (*Müssen* = must)'. So Korngold, let's say in a *Feuilleton* about Richard Strauss, would be able to prove, with a witty parody of Bienenfeld's aphorism and Schönberg's as well, that Art comes neither from ability nor from necessity, but from income (*Einkommen*).

Whatever the difference of opinion about the origin of the word *Art*, one thing is certain: *Criticism* that breeds such excrescences in *all* directions as I have hinted at in my appraisal of these two articles—*really only hinted at*—criticism that is so corrupt, however well it may serve its authors, can only be derived, by God! from *inability*, that is, from unprecedented incapacity and impotence, and the best one can wish for such criticism is what that criticism seems to wish for Art itself, namely: *that it perish (Umkommen).*[41]

ALBAN BERG

TEXT REFERENCES

PART II

'WOZZECK'

1 Today the omitted scenes seem perfectly expendable to us. Berg himself, however, was very sorry about one scene which he had to omit for drama, tic reasons; he placed great value on the episode in question: it is the scene where Wozzeck purchases the murder knife from a Jew's junk shop.

2 The analysis contained in this chapter shows that the opera can be considered throughout as a 'music-drama' in the Wagnerian sense—clear evidence of Berg's endeavour to 'guarantee' his compositional method from several points of view: by reinterpreting the scenic processes in terms of musical architecture, and by the leitmotivic structure of the thematic action.

3 The vocal score of *Wozzeck* by F. H. Klein is widely known, so only a few music examples are given here. Otherwise bar numbers are indicated; where misunderstandings are possible the number of the act in question is added.

4 This is a device that Berg used very frequently throughout his work; it ensures the metrical consistency of whole scenes, even of whole acts.

5 Of this opening Berg said 'The roll was originally intended to empha, size the crescendo between the two chords. That was a purely instru, mental matter, a question of musicality and sonority. But when I heard this part for the first time I discovered, to my immense astonishment, that I could not have set the tone for the work's military milieu more preg, nantly and more simply than with this little drum roll.'

6 The following correspondences between the two cadenzas should be noted: bar 53 second half = bar 109; 56 first half = 110; 55 second half = 111; 56 second half = 112–113; 57 first half = 114.

7 This hunting song gave Berg the opportunity of explaining why he found it necessary to introduce a folk-song element, i.e. to set up a relation in the opera between art music and folk music—something that was the

most natural thing in the world in tonal music. With this so-called 'atonal' harmony it was not easy to make that difference of level quite clear. It was only achieved by filling everything that was to extend into the sphere of the 'popular' with an easily assimilable primitiveness, in so far as this was applicable within the atonal harmony. The following points may be cited: a preference for symmetrical construction of periods and phrases, exploitation of a harmony of thirds and particularly fourths, and melodic writing that makes extensive use of the whole-tone scale and the perfect fourth (whereas usually in the atonal music of the Viennese school the diminished and augmented intervals predominate). So-called 'polytonality' is another such means to more primitive harmonic music-making.

8 The first five notes of the viola solo are also the same as bars 329–332 of the military March.

9 Long after *Wozzeck* was finished Berg wanted to find out about the origin of the word 'Passacaglia'. He looked it up in Riemann's *Lexikon* and found a reference to the synonymous expression 'Folia'. There he read to his great satisfaction: 'The Folia (*idée fixe*) is apparently one of the oldest forms of ostinato.' So, quite unconsciously, he had fulfilled even the verbal sense of the concept!

10 A1 = bars 171–203; a1 = 204–217; b = 218–237; a2 = 238–257; A2 = 258–285.

11 Berg said of the music in this scene: 'There are passages in the Ländler and in the other pieces of dance music that may seem dissonant in a different sense from that characteristic of purely tonal music. They have a dissonance as of several pieces of music in different keys sounding together. This dissonance which obviously grows out of primitive "polytonality" is introduced quite consciously of course, and can be justified not only in terms of the scenic situation but also in terms of musical logic. An example: according to the text books of form, the first period of a Ländler in G minor can either move to the dominant D major or return to the tonic. The confusion of the sequel results from the fact that here it does both (who could take this amiss from a drunkenly extemporizing public house band!). The musicians who modulated to the dominant find their way back, all in order, to the tonic, in bar 429, while the others, equally legitimately, modulate to the relative major key, E-flat major. It is a wonder that they all end up together at the end of the Ländler (bar 447)!'

12 This development, notated in 3/4 time throughout, has a very peculiar metrical structure from bar 692 onwards: in bars 692–696 the 4/8 motif F E-flat D F is transformed into a sort of 5/8 metre until it repeats; in bars 697–703 the 6/8 motif E B-flat A-flat F-sharp G E is transformed into a sort of 7/8 metre, and so on, until 13/8 metre is reached. By including a quaver rest in each case the ingenious rhythmic shifting is brought to a conclusion in bar 736.

13 A remark of Berg's on the subject of this scene: 'It is clear that such music based solely on harmonic and chordal juxtaposition—despite all melodic re-interpretation—has a strongly impressionistic flavour. Really this is quite natural with dramatic events that lead directly into purely natural phenomena (for example the waves of the pond that close over the drowning Wozzeck, the croaking of the toads, the moonrise, etc.). Nevertheless I never wanted to obtain an effect based merely on the colours; everything is constructed according to strict musical principles, and the passage is rich in thematic references to earlier material.'

14 The beginning of this Adagio was part of a symphony that Berg was working on in 1913–14. The inclusion of this passage on *Wozzeck* was the result of a suggestion made by Frau Helene Berg.

CHAMBER CONCERTO FOR PIANO AND VIOLIN WITH THIRTEEN WIND INSTRUMENTS

15 Namely A D S C H B E G, A E B E and A B A B E G. (Note: in the German notation B= B-flat, H= B-natural, and S (Es)= E-flat.)

16 This movement also takes about fifteen minutes to play (including repeat). So the total duration is approximately thirty-nine minutes.

LULU

17 Kraus reprinted the speech, with some additions, in 'Die Fackel' No. 691–695, July 1925, and again as the opening piece in his collection 'Literatur und Lüge', Vienna 1929.

18 At the première of the opera (Zürich, 2nd June 1937) it became evident that the transitional music runs too quickly to permit of a clearly comprehensible film sequence. In later performances the film was generally replaced by projected images showing the most important stages of the intervening action.

19 Besides the congruent elements of the main events listed here opposite one another (such as: trial—medical council, arrest—liberation), smaller

congruences of detail should also be shown, such as: revolver—stetho⁄ scope, bullets—phials, Law—Medicine, paragraph sign—cholera bacilli, chains—bandages, prison clothes—hospital smock, prison corridors— hospital corridors, etc. Also personal correspondences, such as: judge and jury—doctor and students, police—nurses, etc.

20 'Konfession' (No. 10 of the *Lautenlieder*).

21 Sketch letter of 28th August 1934, first and second paragraphs.

22 Schönberg's sixtieth birthday.

VIOLIN CONCERTO

23 The numbers in brackets correspond to the bar numbers in the score. The letters A B C indicate the various formal elements of each section.

24 A kind of ternary form is also indicated in the last section by the double barlines inserted by Berg: (136–157), (158–213), (214–230).

25 This dismantling of the serial chord into the Chorale melody is paralleled in the dismantling of the main rhythm of the cadenza into the rhythm of the Chorale.

26 The instrumentation of the orchestra also serves this simplicity: besides the four horns, Berg requires only double winds, augmented by alto saxophone, double bassoon and bass tuba; the remainder is the usual string quintet, plus harp and percussion. This simplified instrumentation finds characteristic expression in the frequent use of homogeneous sounds.

PART III

WHY IS SCHÖNBERG'S MUSIC SO DIFFICULT TO UNDERSTAND?

27 An expression that Schönberg also uses—independently of Reger— with reference to the language of his own music.

28 *Arnold Schönberg* by Egon Wellesz.

29 Having recognized that the sixth bar is a variant of the third, and that the seventh is nothing other than a variant of the preceding bar, the feeling for musical relationships (without which music would be sense⁄ less) will quickly adjust itself.

30 I dare to cite as an example—without knowing a note of it: any passage of the Wind Quintet that is nearing its completion this summer

of 1924 in the same place (what a coincidence!) where the Quartet in D minor was begun, exactly twenty years ago.

THE MUSICAL IMPOTENCE OF HANS PFITZNER'S 'NEW AESTHETIC'

31 This and all the following quotations are taken from Hans Pfitzner's book *Die neue Aesthetik der musikalischen Impotenz. Ein Verwesungssymptom?* (The New Aesthetic of Musical Impotence. A Sympton of Decay?)

32 An allusion to a phrase of Goethe's: 'Bilde, Künstler, rede nicht, nur ein Hauch sei dein Gedicht.'

33 A play on the words *weinselig* (wine‐happy) and *feinseelig* (fine‐souled). [Trans.]

34 It does happen in Schumann! But not here! Look, for example, to remain in the *Kinderszenen*, at the ending of the fourth piece 'Bittendes Kind' on the chord of the dominant seventh, and the ending of the twelfth piece 'Kind im Einschlummern' which really does lose itself melodically, and finally disappears on a long held sub‐dominant after a ritardando and diminuendo lasting several bars.

TWO FEUILLETONS

35 The evening paper of 7th August 1920: 'Dr Leopold Schmidt' by Julius Korngold.

36 *Neue Freie Presse* morning paper of 17th July 1920.

37 A play on the words *reizen* (in the sense of 'to charm or attract') and *aufreizen* ('to provoke'). [Trans.]

38 Dr Elsa Bienenfeld in the *Neues Wiener Journal* of 17th July 1920.

39 *Neues Wiener Journal* of 11th July 1920.

40 Musical Pocketbook 1911.

41 The German words in brackets are intended to give the gist of the word‐play in the last two paragraphs. [Trans.]

SELECTED BIBLIOGRAPHY

Willi Reich, *Wozzeck. A Guide to the Words and Music of the Opera by Alban Berg.* New York (The League of Composers), 1931. 2nd ed. New York (G. Schirmers Inc.), 1952

Willi Reich, *Alban Berg.* With Berg's own writings and essays by Th. W. Adorno and Ernst Krenek. Vienna (Verlag Herbert Reichner), 1937

Pierre Jean Jouve and Michel Fano, *Wozzeck ou le Nouvel Opéra.* Paris (Librairie Plon), 1953

H. F. Redlich, *Alban Berg. The Man and his Music.* London (John Calder), 1957. Vienna (Universal Edition), 1957

Alban Berg. *Ecrits. Choisis, traduits et commentés par Henri Pousseur.* Monaco (Éditions du Rocher), 1957

Konrad Vogelsang, *Alban Berg. Leben und Werk.* Vol. 5 of Hesse's 'Kleine Bücherei'. Berlin-Halensee (Max Hesses Verlag), 1959

Willi Reich, *Alban Berg. Bildnis im Wort. Selbstzeugnisse und Aussagen der Freunde.* Zürich (Verlag 'Die Arche'), 1959

The author would like to thank Universal Edition, Vienna, the publishers of all Berg's works, for the encouragement which they have given the author's publications on the composer.

LIST OF ILLUSTRATIONS

INDEX

Numbers in italics refer to illustrations